SOUPS

pil

Publications International, Ltd.

Photographs on front cover, page 3 and page 135 © Shutterstock.com. All other photographs copyright © Publications International, Ltd.

Pictured on the front cover: Creamy Tomato Soup *(page 134).*

Pictured on the back cover *(clockwise from top left):* Beef Vegetable Soup *(page 40),* Curried Ginger Pumpkin Soup *(page 123),* Chicken and Gnocchi Soup *(page 6),* One-Pot Chinese Chicken Soup *(page 148),* Broccoli Cheese Soup *(page 140),* Middle Eastern Lentil Soup *(page 106),* Salsa Verde Chicken Soup *(page 147)* and Peppery Sicilian Chicken Soup *(page 5).*

ISBN: 978-1-64558-430-8

Manufactured in China.

8 7 6 5 4 3 2 1

Microwave Cooking: Microwave ovens vary in wattage. Use the cooking times as guidelines and check for doneness before adding more time.

Let's get social!

 @Publications_International

@PublicationsInternational

www.pilbooks.com

CONTENTS

POULTRY

Peppery Sicilian Chicken Soup

2 tablespoons olive oil

1 onion, chopped

1 green bell pepper, chopped

3 stalks celery, chopped

3 carrots, chopped

3 cloves garlic, minced

1 tablespoon salt

3 containers (32 ounces each) chicken broth

2 pounds boneless skinless chicken breasts

1 can (28 ounces) diced tomatoes

2 baking potatoes, peeled and cut into ¼-inch pieces

1½ teaspoons ground white pepper*

1½ teaspoons ground black pepper

½ cup chopped fresh parsley

8 ounces uncooked ditalini pasta

Or substitute additional black pepper for the white pepper.

1. Heat oil in large saucepan or Dutch oven over medium heat. Stir in onion, bell pepper, celery and carrots. Reduce heat to medium-low; cover and cook 10 to 15 minutes or until vegetables are tender but not browned, stirring occasionally. Stir in garlic and 1 tablespoon salt; cover and cook 5 minutes.

2. Stir in broth, chicken, tomatoes, potatoes, white pepper and black pepper; bring to a boil. Reduce heat to low; cover and simmer 1 hour. Remove chicken to plate; set aside until cool enough to handle. Shred chicken and return to saucepan with parsley.

3. Meanwhile, cook pasta in medium saucepan of boiling salted water 7 minutes (or 1 minute less than package directs for al dente). Drain pasta and add to soup. Taste and season with additional salt, if desired.

Chicken and Gnocchi Soup

¼ cup (½ stick) butter

1 tablespoon extra virgin olive oil

1 cup finely diced onion

2 stalks celery, finely chopped

2 cloves garlic, minced

¼ cup all-purpose flour

4 cups half-and-half

1 can (about 14 ounces) chicken broth

1 teaspoon salt

½ teaspoon dried thyme

½ teaspoon dried parsley flakes

¼ teaspoon ground nutmeg

1 package (about 16 ounces) uncooked gnocchi

1 package (6 ounces) fully cooked chicken strips, chopped *or* 1 cup diced cooked chicken

1 cup shredded carrots

1 cup coarsely chopped fresh spinach

1. Melt butter in large saucepan or Dutch oven over medium heat; add oil. Add onion, celery and garlic; cook about 8 minutes or until vegetables are softened and onion is translucent, stirring occasionally.

2. Whisk in flour; cook and stir about 1 minute. Whisk in half-and-half; cook about 15 minutes or until thickened, stirring occasionally.

3. Whisk in broth, salt, thyme, parsley flakes and nutmeg; cook 10 minutes or until soup is slightly thickened, stirring occasionally. Add gnocchi, chicken, carrots and spinach; cook about 5 minutes or until gnocchi are heated through.

Chicken Enchilada Soup

2 tablespoons vegetable oil, divided

1½ pounds boneless skinless chicken breasts, cut into ½-inch pieces

½ cup chopped onion

2 cloves garlic, minced

2 cans (about 14 ounces each) chicken broth

3 cups water, divided

1 cup masa harina

1 package (16 ounces) pasteurized process cheese product, cubed

1 can (10 ounces) mild red enchilada sauce

1 teaspoon chili powder

½ teaspoon salt

½ teaspoon ground cumin

1 large tomato, seeded and chopped

Crispy tortilla strips*

*If tortilla strips are not available, crumble tortilla chips into bite-size pieces.

1. Heat 1 tablespoon oil in large saucepan or Dutch oven over medium-high heat. Add chicken; cook and stir 10 minutes or until no longer pink. Transfer to large bowl with slotted spoon; drain fat from saucepan.

2. Heat remaining 1 tablespoon oil in same saucepan over medium-high heat. Add onion and garlic; cook and stir 3 minutes or until softened. Stir in broth.

3. Whisk 2 cups water into masa harina in large bowl until smooth. Whisk mixture into broth in saucepan. Stir in cheese product, remaining 1 cup water, enchilada sauce, chili powder, salt and cumin; bring to a boil over high heat. Add chicken. Reduce heat to medium-low; simmer 30 minutes, stirring frequently. Top with tomato and tortilla strips.

Turkey Vegetable Rice Soup

1½ pounds turkey drumsticks
(2 small)

8 cups cold water

1 medium onion, cut into
quarters

2 tablespoons soy sauce

¼ teaspoon black pepper

1 bay leaf

2 carrots, sliced

⅓ cup uncooked rice

4 ounces mushrooms, sliced

1 cup fresh snow peas,
cut in half crosswise

1 cup coarsely chopped
bok choy

1. Place turkey in large saucepan or Dutch oven. Add water, onion, soy sauce, pepper and bay leaf; bring to a boil over high heat. Reduce heat to medium-low; simmer, uncovered, 1½ hours or until turkey is tender.

2. Remove turkey to plate; set aside until cool enough to handle. Let broth cool slightly; skim fat. Remove and discard bay leaf. Remove turkey meat from bones; discard skin and bones. Cut turkey into bite-size pieces.

3. Add carrots and rice to broth in saucepan; bring to a boil over high heat. Reduce heat to medium-low; cook 10 minutes.

4. Add mushrooms and turkey to soup; bring to a boil over high heat. Reduce heat to medium-low; cook 5 minutes. Add snow peas and bok choy; bring to a boil over high heat. Reduce heat to medium-low; cook 8 minutes or until rice and vegetables are tender.

Coconut Curry Chicken Soup

3 cups chicken broth

8 boneless skinless chicken thighs

1 cup chopped onion, divided

1 teaspoon salt, divided

4 whole cloves

1 tablespoon butter

2 tablespoons curry powder

1¼ cups coconut milk

¼ cup plus 1 tablespoon chopped fresh mint, divided

3 tablespoons chopped crystallized ginger

¼ teaspoon ground cloves

1½ cups half-and-half

3 cups cooked rice (optional)

Lime wedges (optional)

1. Bring broth to a boil in large skillet over high heat. Add chicken, ½ cup onion, ½ teaspoon salt and whole cloves; return to a boil. Reduce heat to low; cover and simmer 40 minutes or until chicken is very tender.

2. Remove chicken to plate; set aside. Reserve 1 cup cooking liquid in bowl or measuring cup; discard remaining liquid, onion and cloves. Melt butter in same skillet over medium-high heat. Add remaining ½ cup onion; cook and stir 4 minutes or until onion is translucent. Sprinkle curry powder over onions; cook about 20 seconds or just until fragrant, stirring constantly.

3. Add coconut milk, 1 tablespoon mint, ginger, ground cloves and reserved cooking liquid to skillet; cover and cook 10 minutes. Add chicken; cover and cook 15 minutes. Stir in half-and-half and remaining ½ teaspoon salt. Shred chicken slightly, pressing down with a spoon. Cook 1 minute or until heated through. Sprinkle with remaining ¼ cup mint.

4. Spoon rice over each serving, if desired; garnish with lime wedges.

Cock-A-Leekie Soup

4 cups reduced-sodium chicken broth

4 cups water

2½ pounds bone-in skin-on chicken thighs

3 stalks celery, sliced

2 bay leaves

5 to 6 large leeks (about 2½ pounds)

½ cup uncooked pearl barley

1 teaspoon salt

1 teaspoon ground allspice

12 pitted prunes, halved

Black pepper

1. Combine broth, water, chicken, celery and bay leaves in large saucepan or Dutch oven; bring to a boil over high heat. Reduce heat to low; cover and simmer 30 minutes or until chicken is tender. Remove chicken to cutting board to cool.

2. Meanwhile, trim leeks. Cut off roots, any damaged leaves and very tough tops. Cut in half lengthwise, then cut crosswise into ¾-inch pieces. Wash well in several changes of water.

3. Add leeks, barley, 1 teaspoon salt and allspice to saucepan; cover and simmer 40 minutes or until leeks and barley are tender.

4. Remove chicken meat from bones; discard skin and bones. Cut chicken into bite-size pieces. Add chicken to soup with prunes; cook 3 minutes or until prunes soften. Remove and discard bay leaves. Season with additional salt and pepper.

Pozole

1 large onion, thinly sliced

1 tablespoon olive oil

2 teaspoons dried oregano

1 clove garlic, minced

½ teaspoon ground cumin

2 cans (about 14 ounces each) chicken broth

1 package (10 ounces) frozen corn

2 cans (4 ounces each) chopped green chiles, undrained

1 can (2¼ ounces) sliced black olives, drained

¼ teaspoon salt

12 ounces boneless skinless chicken breasts

Chopped fresh cilantro (optional)

1. Combine onion, oil, oregano, garlic and cumin in large saucepan or Dutch oven; cover and cook over low heat about 6 minutes or until onion is tender, stirring occasionally.

2. Add broth, corn, chiles, olives and salt to saucepan; cover and bring to a boil over high heat.

3. Meanwhile, cut chicken into thin strips. Add to soup; cover and cook over medium-low heat 3 to 4 minutes or until chicken is cooked through. Garnish with cilantro.

Cajun-Style Chicken Soup

1½ pounds bone-in skin-on chicken thighs

4 cups chicken broth

1 can (8 ounces) tomato sauce

1 medium onion, chopped

2 stalks celery, sliced

2 cloves garlic, minced

2 bay leaves

1 teaspoon salt

½ teaspoon ground cumin

¼ teaspoon paprika

¼ teaspoon ground red pepper

¼ teaspoon black pepper

Dash white pepper

1 large green bell pepper, chopped

⅓ cup uncooked rice

8 ounces fresh or frozen okra, cut into ½-inch slices

Hot pepper sauce (optional)

1. Combine chicken, broth, tomato sauce, onion, celery, garlic, bay leaves, salt, cumin, paprika, ground red pepper, black pepper and white pepper in large saucepan or Dutch oven; bring to a boil over high heat. Reduce heat to medium-low; simmer, uncovered, 1 hour or until chicken is tender, skimming foam that rises to the surface.

2. Remove chicken from soup; cool slightly. Skim fat from soup. Remove chicken meat from bones; discard skin and bones. Cut chicken into bite-size pieces.

3. Add chicken, bell pepper and rice to soup; bring to a boil. Reduce heat to low; cook, uncovered, about 12 minutes or until rice is tender. Add okra; cook 8 minutes or until okra is tender. Remove and discard bay leaves.

4. Serve soup with hot pepper sauce, if desired.

Chicken and Corn Chowder

1 tablespoon olive oil

1 pound boneless skinless chicken breasts, cut into ½-inch pieces

3 cups thawed frozen corn

¾ cup coarsely chopped onion (about 1 medium)

1 to 2 tablespoons water

1 cup diced carrots

2 tablespoons finely chopped jalapeño pepper* (optional)

½ teaspoon dried oregano

¼ teaspoon dried thyme

3 cups reduced-sodium chicken broth

1½ cups milk

½ teaspoon salt

Jalapeño peppers can sting and irritate the skin, so wear rubber gloves when handling peppers and do not touch your eyes.

1. Heat oil in large saucepan over medium heat. Add chicken; cook and stir about 10 minutes or until browned and no longer pink in center. Remove to plate.

2. Add corn and onion to saucepan; cook and stir about 5 minutes or until onion is tender. Transfer 1 cup corn mixture to food processor or blender; process until finely chopped, adding water to liquify if necessary.

3. Add carrots, jalapeño, if desired, oregano and thyme to saucepan; cook and stir about 5 minutes or until corn begins to brown. Return chicken to saucepan. Stir in broth, milk, chopped corn mixture and salt; bring to a boil. Reduce heat to low; cover and simmer 15 to 20 minutes.

Tortilla Soup

Vegetable oil

3 (6- or 7-inch) corn tortillas, halved and cut into strips

½ cup chopped onion

1 clove garlic, minced

2 cans (about 14 ounces each) chicken broth

1 can (about 14 ounces) diced tomatoes

1 cup shredded cooked chicken

2 teaspoons fresh lime juice

1 small avocado, diced

2 tablespoons chopped fresh cilantro

1. Pour ½ inch oil into small skillet; heat to 360°F over medium-high heat. Add tortilla strips, a few at a time; cook 1 minute or until crisp and lightly browned. Remove with slotted spoon; drain on paper towel-lined plate.*

2. Heat 2 teaspoons oil in large saucepan over medium heat. Add onion and garlic; cook and stir 6 minutes or until onion is softened. Add broth and tomatoes; bring to a boil. Reduce heat to low; cover and simmer 15 minutes.

3. Add chicken and lime juice; cook 5 minutes. Top soup with tortilla strips, avocado and cilantro.

*To save time, purchase packaged crispy tortilla strips at the grocery store (found in the snack aisle or with salad toppings) and skip step 1.

Mulligatawny Soup

1 tablespoon olive oil

1 pound boneless skinless chicken breasts, cut into ½-inch pieces

2 cups finely chopped carrots

1 cup chopped green bell pepper

2 stalks celery, thinly sliced

½ cup finely chopped onion

3 cloves garlic, minced

¼ cup all-purpose flour

1 to 2 teaspoons curry powder

¼ teaspoon ground nutmeg

3 cups chicken broth

1 cup milk

1 cup chopped seeded tomato

1 medium apple, peeled and sliced

¼ cup uncooked converted rice

½ teaspoon salt

⅛ teaspoon black pepper

1. Heat oil in large saucepan over medium heat. Add chicken, carrots, bell pepper, celery, onion and garlic; cook and stir 5 minutes. Sprinkle with flour, curry powder and nutmeg; cook and stir 1 to 2 minutes.

2. Stir in broth, milk, tomato, apple, rice, salt and black pepper; bring to a boil over medium-high heat. Reduce heat to low; cover and simmer 20 minutes or until rice is tender.

Turkey Albondigas Soup

½ cup uncooked brown rice

MEATBALLS

1 pound ground turkey

2 tablespoons minced onion

2 teaspoons chopped fresh cilantro

2 teaspoons milk

1 teaspoon hot pepper sauce

¼ teaspoon dried oregano

¼ teaspoon black pepper

BROTH

1 tablespoon olive oil

¼ cup chopped onion

2 cloves garlic, minced

5 cups chicken broth

1 tablepoon hot pepper sauce

1 teaspoon tomato paste

¼ teaspoon black pepper

3 medium carrots, cut into ¼-inch slices (about 2 cups)

1 medium zucchini, quartered lengthwise and cut crosswise into ½-inch slices

1 yellow squash, quartered lengthwise and cut crosswise into ½-inch slices

Lime wedges

1. Prepare rice according to package directions.

2. Meanwhile, prepare meatballs. Combine turkey, 2 tablespoons minced onion, 2 teaspoons chopped cilantro, milk, 1 teaspoon hot pepper sauce, oregano and ¼ teaspoon black pepper in medium bowl; mix lightly until blended. Shape mixture into 1-inch balls.

3. For broth, heat oil in large saucepan over medium heat. Add ¼ cup chopped onion and garlic; cook and stir until golden brown. Add broth, 1 tablespoon hot pepper sauce, tomato paste and ¼ teaspoon black pepper; bring to a boil over high heat.

4. Reduce heat to low. Add meatballs and carrots to broth; simmer 15 minutes. Add zucchini, squash and cooked rice; simmer 5 to 10 minutes or just until vegetables are tender. Serve immediately with lime wedges.

North African Chicken Soup

¾ teaspoon paprika

½ teaspoon ground ginger

½ teaspoon ground cumin

½ teaspoon ground allspice

8 ounces boneless skinless chicken breasts, cut into ½-inch pieces

1 tablespoon olive oil

2½ cups chicken broth

2 cups peeled sweet potato, cut into ½-inch pieces

1 cup chopped onion

½ cup water

3 cloves garlic, minced

1 teaspoon sugar

2 cups undrained canned tomatoes, coarsely chopped

Black pepper

1. Combine paprika, ginger, cumin and allspice in small bowl; mix well. Combine 1 teaspoon spice mixture and chicken in medium bowl; toss to coat.

2. Heat oil in large saucepan over medium-high heat. Add chicken; cook and stir 3 to 4 minutes or until chicken is cooked through. Remove to plate.

3. Combine broth, sweet potato, onion, water, garlic, sugar and remaining spice mixture in same saucepan; bring to a boil over high heat. Reduce heat to medium-low; cover and simmer 10 minutes or until sweet potato is tender. Stir in tomatoes and chicken; cook until heated through. Season to taste with pepper.

MEAT

Sausage and Lentil Soup

8 ounces bulk hot Italian sausage

1 onion, chopped

2 cloves garlic, minced

1 stalk celery, chopped

1 carrot, chopped

1 small zucchini, chopped

3 to 3½ cups chicken broth, divided

1 can (about 14 ounces) diced tomatoes

1 cup dried lentils, rinsed and sorted

½ teaspoon salt

½ teaspoon dried oregano

½ teaspoon dried basil

¼ teaspoon dried thyme

¼ teaspoon black pepper

Chopped fresh basil and grated Parmesan cheese (optional)

1. Brown sausage in large saucepan or Dutch oven over medium-high heat, stirring to break up meat. Add onion; cook and stir 3 minutes or until onion begins to soften. Add garlic; cook and stir 1 minute. Add celery, carrot and zucchini; cook 3 minutes, stirring occasionally.

2. Stir in 3 cups broth, tomatoes, lentils, salt, oregano, dried basil, thyme and pepper; bring to a boil. Reduce heat to low; cover and simmer about 1 hour or until lentils are tender. Add additional broth, if necessary, to thin soup. Garnish with fresh basil and cheese.

Ginger Wonton Soup

4 ounces ground pork

½ cup ricotta cheese

1½ teaspoons minced fresh cilantro

½ teaspoon black pepper

⅛ teaspoon Chinese five-spice powder

20 wonton wrappers

1 teaspoon vegetable oil

⅓ cup chopped red bell pepper

1 teaspoon grated fresh ginger

2 cans (about 14 ounces each) chicken broth

2 teaspoons reduced-sodium soy sauce

4 ounces fresh snow peas, cut into ½-inch pieces

1 can (about 9 ounces) baby corn, rinsed, drained and halved

2 green onions, thinly sliced

1. Cook pork in small nonstick skillet over medium-high heat 4 minutes or until no longer pink. Cool slightly; stir in ricotta, cilantro, black pepper and five-spice powder.

2. Place 1 teaspoon filling in center of each wonton wrapper. Fold top corner of wonton over filling. Lightly brush remaining corners with water. Fold left and right corners over filling; tightly roll filled end toward remaining corner in jelly-roll fashion. Moisten edges with water to seal. Cover with plastic wrap until ready to cook.

3. Heat oil in large saucepan over medium heat. Add bell pepper and ginger; cook and stir 1 minute. Add broth and soy sauce; bring to a boil. Add snow peas, corn and wontons; cook over medium-low heat 4 to 5 minutes or until wontons are tender. Sprinkle with green onions.

Corned Beef and Cabbage Soup

1 tablespoon vegetable oil

1 onion, chopped

2 stalks celery, chopped

2 carrots, chopped

2 cloves garlic, minced

4 to 5 cups coarsely chopped green cabbage (about half of small head)

12 ounces unpeeled Yukon gold potatoes, chopped

4 cups beef broth

4 cups water

½ cup quick-cooking barley

1 teaspoon salt

1 teaspoon dried thyme

½ teaspoon black pepper

¼ teaspoon ground mustard

12 ounces corned beef, cut into ½-inch pieces (leftovers or deli corned beef, about 2½ cups)

1. Heat oil in large saucepan or Dutch oven over medium-high heat. Add onion, celery and carrots; cook about 5 minutes or until vegetables are softened, stirring occasionally. Add garlic; cook and stir 1 minute.

2. Stir in cabbage, potatoes, broth, water, barley, 1 teaspoon salt, thyme, ½ teaspoon pepper and mustard; bring to a boil. Reduce heat to medium-low; simmer 20 minutes, stirring occasionally.

3. Stir in corned beef; cook 10 to 15 minutes or until potatoes are tender. Season with additional salt and pepper, if desired.

Beef and Beet Borscht

2 cans (15 ounces each) julienned beets

1 cup buttermilk

⅛ teaspoon black pepper

⅛ teaspoon ground cloves

1 cup beef broth

4 ounces thinly sliced deli roast beef, cut into short thin strips

¼ cup sour cream

Chopped fresh parsley (optional)

1. Drain beets, reserving 1 cup liquid. Place half of beets in food processor; process until finely chopped. Add buttermilk, pepper and cloves; process until smooth. Transfer to medium bowl.

2. Stir in remaining beets, broth, reserved beet liquid and roast beef; mix well. Cover and refrigerate at least 2 hours or up to 24 hours. Top with sour cream and parsley, if desired.

Hearty Tuscan Soup

1 teaspoon olive oil

1 pound bulk mild or hot Italian sausage*

1 medium onion, chopped

3 cloves garlic, minced

¼ cup all-purpose flour

5 cups chicken broth

1 teaspoon salt

½ teaspoon Italian seasoning

3 medium unpeeled russet potatoes (about 1 pound), halved lengthwise and thinly sliced

2 cups packed torn stemmed kale leaves

1 cup half-and-half or whipping cream

Or use sausage links and remove from casings.

1. Heat oil in large saucepan or Dutch oven over medium-high heat. Add sausage; cook until sausage begins to brown, stirring to break up meat. Add onion and garlic; cook about 5 minutes or until onion is softened and sausage is browned, stirring occasionally.

2. Stir in flour until blended. Add broth, salt and Italian seasoning; bring to a boil. Stir in potatoes and kale. Reduce heat to medium-low; simmer 15 to 20 minutes or until potatoes are fork-tender. Reduce heat to low; stir in half-and-half. Cook about 5 minutes or until heated through.

Beef Vegetable Soup

1½ pounds cubed beef stew meat

¼ cup all-purpose flour

3 tablespoons vegetable oil, divided

1 onion, chopped

2 stalks celery, chopped

3 tablespoons tomato paste

2 teaspoons salt

1 teaspoon dried thyme

½ teaspoon garlic powder

¼ teaspoon black pepper

6 cups beef broth, divided

1 can (28 ounces) stewed tomatoes, undrained

1 tablespoon Worcestershire sauce

1 bay leaf

4 unpeeled red potatoes (about 1 pound), cut into 1-inch pieces

3 medium carrots, cut in half lengthwise and cut into ½-inch slices

6 ounces green beans, trimmed and cut into 1-inch pieces

1 cup frozen corn

1. Combine beef and flour in medium bowl; toss to coat. Heat 1 tablespoon oil in large saucepan or Dutch oven over medium-high heat. Cook beef in two batches about 5 minutes or until browned on all sides, adding additional 1 tablespoon oil after first batch. Transfer beef to medium bowl.

2. Heat remaining 1 tablespoon oil in same saucepan. Add onion and celery; cook and stir about 5 minutes or until softened. Add tomato paste, 2 teaspoons salt, thyme, garlic powder and ¼ teaspoon pepper; cook and stir 1 minute. Stir in 1 cup broth, scraping up browned bits from bottom of saucepan. Stir in remaining 5 cups broth, tomatoes, Worcestershire sauce, bay leaf and beef; bring to a boil.

3. Reduce heat to low; cover and simmer 1 hour and 20 minutes. Add potatoes and carrots; cook 15 minutes. Add green beans and corn; cook 15 minutes or until vegetables are tender. Remove and discard bay leaf. Season with additional salt and pepper.

Pork and Cabbage Soup

8 ounces pork loin, cut into ½-inch pieces

1 medium onion, chopped

2 slices bacon, finely chopped

1 can (about 28 ounces) whole tomatoes, drained and coarsely chopped

2 cups beef broth

2 cups chicken broth

2 medium carrots, sliced

1 teaspoon salt

1 bay leaf

¾ teaspoon dried marjoram

⅛ teaspoon black pepper

¼ medium cabbage, chopped

2 tablespoons chopped fresh parsley

1. Heat large saucepan or Dutch oven over medium heat. Add pork, onion and bacon; cook and stir until pork is no longer pink and onion is slightly tender.

2. Stir in tomatoes, beef broth, chicken broth, carrots, salt, bay leaf, marjoram and pepper; bring to a boil over high heat. Reduce heat to medium-low; simmer, uncovered, about 30 minutes. Remove and discard bay leaf.

3. Add cabbage; bring to a boil over high heat. Reduce heat to medium-low; simmer, uncovered, about 15 minutes or until cabbage is tender. Stir in parsley.

Italian Wedding Soup

MEATBALLS

- 2 eggs
- 2 cloves garlic, minced
- 1 teaspoon salt
- ⅛ teaspoon black pepper
- 1½ pounds meat loaf mix (ground beef and pork)
- ¾ cup plain dry bread crumbs
- ½ cup grated Parmesan cheese
- 2 tablespoons olive oil

SOUP

- 1 onion, chopped
- 2 carrots, chopped
- 4 cloves garlic, minced
- 2 heads escarole or curly endive, coarsely chopped
- 8 cups chicken broth
- 1 can (about 14 ounces) Italian plum tomatoes, undrained, coarsely chopped
- 3 fresh thyme sprigs
- 1 teaspoon salt
- ½ teaspoon red pepper flakes
- 1 cup uncooked acini di pepe pasta

1. For meatballs, whisk eggs, 2 cloves garlic, 1 teaspoon salt and black pepper in large bowl until blended. Stir in meat loaf mix, bread crumbs and cheese; mix gently until well blended. Shape mixture by tablespoonfuls into 1-inch balls.

2. Heat oil in large saucepan or Dutch oven over medium heat. Cook meatballs in batches 5 minutes or until browned. Remove to plate; set aside.

3. For soup, add onion, carrots and 4 cloves garlic to saucepan; cook and stir 5 minutes or until onion is lightly browned. Add escarole; cook 2 minutes or until wilted. Stir in broth, tomatoes with juice, thyme, 1 teaspoon salt and red pepper flakes; bring to a boil over high heat. Reduce heat to medium-low; cook 15 minutes.

4. Add meatballs and pasta to soup; return to a boil over high heat. Reduce heat to medium; cook 10 minutes or until pasta is tender. Remove and discard thyme sprigs before serving.

Vietnamese Beef Soup (Pho)

12 ounces boneless beef top sirloin or top round steak

4 ounces thin rice noodles (rice sticks)

6 cups beef broth

3 cups water

2 tablespoons minced fresh ginger

2 tablespoons reduced-sodium soy sauce

1 cinnamon stick (3 inches long)

½ cup thinly sliced carrots

2 cups fresh bean sprouts

1 red onion, halved and thinly sliced

½ cup chopped fresh cilantro

½ cup chopped fresh basil

2 minced jalapeño peppers* or 1 to 3 teaspoons chili sauce

*Jalapeño peppers can sting and irritate the skin, so wear rubber gloves when handling peppers and do not touch your eyes.

1. Freeze beef 45 minutes or until firm. Place rice noodles in large bowl. Cover with hot water; soak 20 minutes or until soft. Drain.

2. Meanwhile, combine broth, water, ginger, soy sauce and cinnamon stick in large saucepan; bring to a boil over high heat. Reduce heat to low; cover and simmer 20 minutes. Remove and discard cinnamon stick.

3. Slice beef lengthwise in half, then crosswise into very thin strips. Add noodles and carrots to simmering broth; cook 2 to 3 minutes or until carrots are tender. Add beef and bean sprouts; cook 1 minute or until beef is no longer pink.

4. Remove from heat; stir in onion, cilantro, basil and jalapeños.

Tip

Rice noodles are semi-translucent dried noodles that come in many sizes and have many names, including rice stick noodles, rice-flour noodles and pho noodles. Widths range from very thin (called rice vermicelli) to 1 inch wide. All rice noodles must be soaked to soften before using.

Beef Goulash Soup

1 tablespoon olive oil

1¼ pounds boneless beef sirloin tri-tip roast,* cut into 1-inch pieces

1 cup chopped onion

3 cans (about 14 ounces each) beef broth

2 cans (about 14 ounces each) diced tomatoes

1½ cups sliced carrots

1 tablespoon sugar

1 tablespoon paprika

1 tablespoon caraway seeds, slightly crushed

2 cloves garlic, minced

½ teaspoon salt

4 ounces (about 2 cups) uncooked whole wheat noodles

2 cups thinly sliced cabbage or coleslaw mix

Or substitute chuck roast or beef round steak.

1. Heat oil in large saucepan or Dutch oven over medium heat. Brown beef in two batches; remove to plate. Add onion to saucepan; cook 3 minutes or until onion is tender, stirring occasionally.

2. Return beef to saucepan. Add broth, tomatoes, carrots, sugar, paprika, caraway seeds, garlic and salt; bring to a boil. Reduce heat to medium-low; cover and simmer 45 minutes or until beef is tender.

3. Stir in noodles; bring to a boil. Reduce heat to medium-low; cook, uncovered, 10 minutes or until noodles are tender. Stir in cabbage; cook 2 minutes or until heated through.

Lamb Meatball and Chickpea Soup

1 pound ground lamb

¼ cup chopped onion

1 clove garlic, minced

1 teaspoon ground cumin

½ teaspoon salt

2 cups chicken broth

1 package (10 ounces) frozen chopped broccoli*

1 tomato, peeled and chopped

1 can (about 15 ounces) chickpeas or black-eyed peas, rinsed and drained

½ teaspoon dried thyme

Black pepper

*Or substitute 1½ cups fresh broccoli florets for frozen chopped broccoli.

1. Combine lamb, onion, garlic, cumin and ½ teaspoon salt in medium bowl; mix lightly. Shape into 1-inch balls.** Brown meatballs in large skillet over medium-high heat, turning occasionally.

2. Meanwhile, bring broth to a boil in large saucepan over high heat. Add broccoli and tomato; bring to a boil.

3. Reduce heat to medium-low. Add meatballs, chickpeas and thyme; cover and cook 5 minutes. Season with additional salt and pepper.

**To quickly shape uniform meatballs, place lamb mixture on cutting board; pat evenly into large square about 1 inch thick. Cut into 1-inch squares; shape each square into a ball.

Portuguese Potato and Greens Soup

2 tablespoons olive oil

1 cup chopped onion

1 cup chopped carrots

2 cloves garlic, minced

1 pound unpeeled new red potatoes, cut into 1-inch pieces

2 cups water

1 can (about 14 ounces) chicken broth

8 ounces uncooked Mexican chorizo sausage, casings removed

8 ounces kale

Salt and black pepper

1. Heat oil in large saucepan over medium heat. Add onion, carrots and garlic; cook and stir 5 to 6 minutes or until lightly browned. Add potatoes, water and broth; bring to a boil. Reduce heat to low; cover and simmer 10 to 15 minutes or until potatoes are tender.

2. Meanwhile, heat large nonstick skillet over medium heat. Crumble chorizo into skillet; cook and stir 5 to 6 minutes or until sausage is cooked through. Drain on paper towel-lined plate.

3. Wash kale; remove tough stems. Cut into thin slices.

4. Add sausage and kale to broth mixture; cook over medium heat 4 to 5 minutes or until heated through. (Kale should be bright green and slightly crunchy.) Season with salt and pepper.

SEAFOOD

Creamy Seafood Bisque

2 tablespoons olive oil

1 onion, finely chopped

2 cups chicken broth

1 package (9 ounces) frozen artichoke hearts, thawed

½ cup dry white wine

1 pound mixed shellfish (raw shrimp, peeled and deveined; raw scallops; and/or canned crabmeat)

1 cup whipping cream

2 tablespoons chopped fresh parsley

1 teaspoon salt

½ teaspoon ground nutmeg

¼ teaspoon white pepper

1. Heat oil in large saucepan over medium-high heat. Add onion; cook and stir 5 minutes or until softened. Add broth, artichokes and wine; bring to a boil over medium-high heat. Reduce heat to low; cover and simmer 5 to 7 minutes.

2. Working in batches, process soup in food processor or blender until smooth. (Or use hand-held immersion blender.) Return soup to saucepan.

3. Stir in shellfish, cream, parsley, salt, nutmeg and pepper; bring to a simmer over medium heat. Reduce heat to low; simmer, uncovered, 5 to 10 minutes. *Do not boil.* (Shellfish will become tough if soup boils.)

Spicy Thai Shrimp Soup

1 tablespoon vegetable oil

1 pound medium raw shrimp, peeled and deveined, shells reserved

1 jalapeño pepper,* cut into slivers

1 tablespoon paprika

¼ teaspoon ground red pepper

4 cans (about 14 ounces each) chicken broth

1 (½-inch) strip *each* lemon and lime peel

1 can (15 ounces) straw mushrooms, drained

Juice of 1 lemon

Juice of 1 lime

2 tablespoons soy sauce

1 red Thai pepper* or red jalapeño pepper* *or* ¼ small red bell pepper, cut into strips

¼ cup fresh cilantro leaves

Chile peppers can sting and irritate the skin, so wear rubber gloves when handling peppers and do not touch your eyes.

1. Heat large skillet or wok over medium-high heat 1 minute. Add oil; heat 30 seconds. Add shrimp and jalapeño; stir-fry 1 minute. Add paprika and ground red pepper; stir-fry 1 minute or until shrimp turn pink and opaque. Transfer shrimp mixture to medium bowl.

2. Add shrimp shells to skillet; cook and stir 30 seconds. Add broth and lemon and lime peels; bring to a boil. Reduce heat to low; cover and simmer 15 minutes.

3. Remove and discard shells and peels with slotted spoon. Add mushrooms and shrimp mixture to broth; bring to a boil over medium heat. Stir in lemon and lime juices, soy sauce and Thai pepper; cook until heated through. Sprinkle with cilantro. Serve immediately.

Cioppino

1 tablespoon olive oil

1 large onion, chopped

1 cup sliced celery

1 clove garlic, minced

4 cups water

1 tablespoon Italian seasoning

1 cube fish-flavored bouillon

4 ounces cod or other boneless mild-flavored fish fillets, cut into ½-inch pieces

1 large tomato, chopped

1 can (10 ounces) baby clams, rinsed and drained (optional)

4 ounces small raw shrimp, peeled and deveined

4 ounces raw bay scallops

¼ cup flaked crabmeat or crabmeat blend

2 tablespoons lemon juice

1. Heat oil in large saucepan over medium heat. Add onion, celery and garlic; cook and stir 5 minutes or until onion is softened.

2. Add water, Italian seasoning and bouillon; bring to a boil over high heat. Stir in fish and tomato. Reduce heat to medium-low; cook about 5 minutes or until fish is opaque.

3. Add clams, if desired, shrimp, scallops, crabmeat and lemon juice; cook about 5 minutes or until shrimp and scallops turn opaque.

Savory Seafood Soup

2½ cups water or chicken broth

1½ cups dry white wine

1 onion, chopped

½ red bell pepper, chopped

½ green bell pepper, chopped

1 clove garlic, minced

8 ouces halibut, cut into 1-inch pieces

8 ounces sea scallops, cut into halves

1 teaspoon dried thyme

Juice of ½ lime

Dash hot pepper sauce

Salt and black pepper

1. Combine water, wine, onion, bell peppers and garlic in large saucepan; bring to a boil over high heat. Reduce heat to medium-low; cover and simmer 15 minutes or until bell peppers are tender, stirring occasionally.

2. Add fish, scallops and thyme; cook 2 minutes or until fish and scallops turn opaque.

3. Stir in lime juice and hot pepper sauce; season with salt and black pepper.

Tips

If halibut is not available, substitute cod, ocean perch or haddock. When buying fresh fish, store it tightly wrapped in the refrigerator and use within 2 days of purchase.

Shrimp Bisque

¼ cup (½ stick) butter

1 pound medium raw shrimp, peeled, deveined and coarsely chopped into ½-inch pieces

2 large green onions, sliced

1 clove garlic, minced

¼ cup all-purpose flour

1 cup chicken broth

3 cups half-and-half

½ teaspoon salt

½ teaspoon grated lemon peel

Pinch ground red pepper

2 tablespoons dry white wine (optional)

Additional whole shrimp (optional)

1. Melt butter in large saucepan over medium heat. Add shrimp, green onions and garlic; cook and stir until shrimp turn pink and opaque. Remove from heat.

2. Add flour; cook and stir just until bubbly. Stir in broth; cook 3 minutes, stirring constantly. Remove from heat.

3. Process soup in small batches in food processor or blender until smooth. (Or use hand-held immersion blender.) Return soup to saucepan.

4. Stir in half-and-half, salt, lemon peel, red pepper and wine, if desired; cook until heated through. Garnish, if desired.

New Orleans Fish Soup

1 can (about 15 ounces)
 cannellini beans,
 rinsed and drained

1 can (about 14 ounces)
 chicken broth

1 yellow squash, halved
 lengthwise and sliced (1 cup)

1 tablespoon Cajun seasoning

2 cans (about 14 ounces each)
 stewed tomatoes

1 pound skinless firm fish fillets,
 such as grouper, cod or
 haddock, cut into 1-inch
 pieces

½ cup sliced green onions

1 teaspoon grated orange peel

1. Combine beans, broth, squash and Cajun seasoning in large saucepan; bring to a boil over high heat.

2. Stir in tomatoes and fish. Reduce heat to medium-low; cover and cook 3 to 5 minutes or until fish begins to flake when tested with fork. Stir in green onions and orange peel.

New England Clam Chowder

1 tablespoon vegetable oil

4 ounces smoked sausage, finely chopped

1½ cups chopped onions

2¾ cups milk

1 medium red potato, diced

1 can (6½ ounces) minced clams, drained, liquid reserved

2 bay leaves

½ teaspoon dried thyme

2 tablespoons butter

¼ teaspoon black pepper

15 saltine crackers

1. Heat oil in large saucepan over medium-high heat. Add sausage; cook and stir 2 minutes or until browned. Remove to plate.

2. Add onions to saucepan; cook and stir 2 minutes. Stir in milk, potato, reserved clam liquid, bay leaves and thyme. Reduce heat to medium-low; cover and simmer 15 minutes or until potato is tender.

3. Remove and discard bay leaves. Add sausage, clams, butter and pepper; cook until heated through, stirring frequently.

4. Crumble crackers over soup just before serving.

Spicy Shrimp Gumbo

½ cup vegetable oil

½ cup all-purpose flour

1 large onion, chopped

½ cup chopped fresh parsley

½ cup chopped celery

½ cup sliced green onions

6 cloves garlic, minced

4 cups chicken broth or water*

1 package (10 ounces) frozen sliced okra, thawed (optional)

1 teaspoon salt

½ teaspoon ground red pepper

2 pounds medium raw shrimp, peeled and deveined

3 cups hot cooked rice

Fresh parsley sprigs (optional)

Traditional gumbo is thick like stew. For thinner gumbo, add 1 to 2 cups additional broth.

1. For roux, blend oil and flour in large saucepan or Dutch oven until smooth. Cook over medium heat 10 to 15 minutes or until roux is dark brown but not burned, stirring frequently.

2. Add chopped onion, chopped parsley, celery, green onions and garlic to roux; cook 5 to 10 minutes or until vegetables are tender. Add broth, okra, if desired, salt and red pepper; cover and cook 15 minutes.

3. Add shrimp; cook 3 to 5 minutes or until shrimp turn pink and opaque.

4. Place about ⅓ cup rice into eight soup bowls; top with gumbo. Garnish with parsley.

Mediterranean Fish Soup

- 4 ounces uncooked pastina or other small pasta
- 1 tablespoon olive oil
- ¾ cup chopped onion
- 2 cloves garlic, minced
- 1 teaspoon whole fennel seeds
- 1 can (about 14 ounces) stewed tomatoes
- 1 can (about 14 ounces) chicken broth
- 1 tablespoon minced fresh Italian parsley
- ½ teaspoon salt
- ½ teaspoon black pepper
- ¼ teaspoon ground turmeric
- 8 ounces firm white fish, cut into 1-inch pieces
- 3 ounces small raw shrimp, peeled (with tails on)

1. Cook pasta according to package directions. Drain pasta; cover and keep warm.

2. Meanwhile, heat oil in large saucepan over medium heat. Add onion, garlic and fennel seeds; cook and stir 3 minutes or until onion is crisp-tender.

3. Stir in tomatoes, broth, parsley, salt, pepper and turmeric; bring to a boil. Reduce heat to low; simmer, uncovered, 10 minutes.

4. Add fish to saucepan; cook 1 minute. Add shrimp; cook just until shrimp turn pink and opaque. Divide pasta evenly among four bowls; ladle soup over pasta.

Shrimp, Mushroom and Omelet Soup

MAKES 6 SERVINGS

10 to 12 dried shiitake mushrooms (about 1 ounce)

3 eggs

1 tablespoon chopped fresh chives or minced green onion tops

2 teaspoons vegetable oil

3 cans (about 14 ounces each) chicken broth

2 tablespoons oyster sauce

12 ounces medium raw shrimp, peeled and deveined

3 cups lightly packed stemmed fresh spinach

1 tablespoon lime juice

Red pepper flakes and grated lime peel (optional)

1. Place mushrooms in bowl; cover with hot water. Let stand 30 minutes or until caps are soft.

2. Meanwhile, whisk eggs and chives in small bowl until blended. Heat 10- to 12-inch nonstick skillet over medium-high heat. Add oil; swirl to coat surface. Pour egg mixture into skillet. Reduce heat to medium; cover and cook, without stirring, 2 minutes or until set on bottom. Slide spatula under omelet; lift omelet and tilt pan to allow uncooked egg to flow underneath. Repeat at several places around omelet.

3. Slide omelet onto flat plate. Hold another plate over omelet and turn omelet over. Slide omelet back into skillet to cook second side about 20 seconds. Slide back onto plate. When cool enough to handle, roll up omelet; cut into ¼-inch-wide strips.

4. Drain mushrooms; squeeze out excess water. Remove and discard stems; slice caps into thin strips.

5. Combine mushrooms, broth and oyster sauce in large saucepan; bring to a boil over high heat. Reduce heat to low; cook 5 minutes. Add shrimp; cook over medium-high heat 2 minutes or until shrimp turn pink and opaque. Add omelet strips and spinach; remove from heat. Cover and let stand 1 to 2 minutes or until spinach wilts slightly. Stir in lime juice. Garnish with red pepper flakes and lime peel.

PASTA & NOODLES

Chicken Noodle Soup

2 tablespoons butter

1 cup chopped onion

1 cup sliced carrots

½ cup diced celery

2 tablespoons vegetable oil

1 pound chicken breast tenderloins

1 pound chicken thigh fillets

4 cups chicken broth, divided

2 cups water

1 tablespoon minced fresh parsley, plus additional for garnish

1½ teaspoons salt

½ teaspoon black pepper

3 cups uncooked egg noodles

1. Melt butter in large saucepan or Dutch oven over medium-low heat. Add onion, carrots and celery; cook 15 minutes or until vegetables are soft, stirring occasionally.

2. Meanwhile, heat oil in large skillet over medium-high heat. Add chicken in single layer; cook about 6 minutes per side or until lightly browned and cooked through. Remove chicken to cutting board. Add 1 cup broth to skillet; cook 1 minute, scraping up browned bits from bottom of skillet. Add broth to vegetables in saucepan. Stir in remaining 3 cups broth, water, 1 tablespoon parsley, salt and pepper.

3. Chop chicken into 1-inch pieces when cool enough to handle. Add to soup; bring to a boil over medium-high heat. Reduce heat to medium-low; simmer, uncovered, 15 minutes. Add noodles; cook 15 minutes or until noodles are tender. Garnish with additional parsley.

Japanese Noodle Soup

1 package (8½ ounces) Japanese udon noodles

1 tablespoon vegetable oil

1 medium red bell pepper, cut into thin strips

1 medium carrot, diagonally sliced

2 green onions, thinly sliced

2 cans (about 14 ounces each) beef broth

1 cup water

1 teaspoon soy sauce

½ teaspoon grated fresh ginger

½ teaspoon black pepper

2 cups thinly sliced fresh shiitake mushrooms, stems discarded

4 ounces daikon (Japanese radish), peeled and cut into thin strips

4 ounces firm tofu, drained and cut into ½-inch cubes

1. Cook noodles according to package directions. Drain and rinse noodles; set aside.

2. Heat oil in large saucepan over medium-high heat. Add bell pepper, carrot and green onions; cook about 3 minutes or until vegetables are slightly softened. Stir in broth, water, soy sauce, ginger and black pepper; bring to a boil. Stir in mushrooms, daikon and tofu. Reduce heat to low; cook 5 minutes.

3. Place noodles in serving bowls; ladle soup over noodles.

Spicy Lentil and Pasta Soup

MAKES 6 SERVINGS

1 tabespoon olive oil

2 medium onions, thinly sliced

½ cup chopped carrot

½ cup chopped celery

½ cup chopped peeled turnip

1 small jalapeño pepper,*
   finely chopped

2 cans (about 14 ounces each)
   vegetable broth

2 cups water

1 can (about 14 ounces)
   stewed tomatoes

8 ounces dried lentils, rinsed
   and sorted

2 teaspoons chili powder

½ teaspoon dried oregano

3 ounces uncooked whole wheat
   spaghetti, broken

2 tablespoons minced fresh
   cilantro

*Jalapeño peppers can sting and irritate
the skin, so wear rubber gloves when
handling peppers and do not touch
your eyes.*

1. Heat oil in large saucepan over medium heat. Add onions, carrot, celery, turnip and jalapeño; cook and stir 10 minutes or until vegetables are crisp-tender.

2. Add broth, water, tomatoes, lentils, chili powder and oregano; bring to a boil. Reduce heat to low; cover and simmer 20 to 30 minutes or until lentils are tender.

3. Add pasta; cook 10 minutes or until tender. Top with cilantro.

Curried Turkey Noodle Soup

MAKES 4 SERVINGS

1 tablespoon olive oil

12 ounces turkey breast tenderloin, cut into bite-size pieces

5 cups water

2 packages (3 ounces each) chicken-flavored ramen noodles

1 tablespoon curry powder

¼ teaspoon salt

1 cup sliced celery

1 medium apple, cored and chopped (1½ cups)

¼ cup dry roasted unsalted peanuts

1. Heat oil in large saucepan over medium-high heat. Add turkey; cook and stir 3 to 4 minutes or until no longer pink. Remove to bowl.

2. Add water, seasoning packets from noodles, curry powder and salt to saucepan; bring to a boil. Reduce heat to low; cover and simmer 5 minutes.

3. Break up noodles. Gently stir noodles and celery into saucepan; bring to a boil. Reduce heat to low; simmer, uncovered, 5 minutes.

4. Stir in turkey and apple; cook until heated through. Top with peanuts.

Italian Pasta Soup with Fennel

1 tablespoon olive oil

1 small fennel bulb, trimmed and chopped into ¼-inch pieces (1½ cups)

4 cloves garlic, minced

3 cups vegetable broth

1 cup uncooked small shell pasta

1 medium zucchini or yellow squash, cut into ½-inch pieces

1 can (about 14 ounces) Italian-seasoned diced tomatoes

¼ cup grated Romano or Parmesan cheese

¼ cup chopped fresh basil

Dash black pepper

1. Heat oil in large saucepan over medium heat. Add fennel; cook and stir 5 minutes. Add garlic; cook and stir 30 seconds. Add broth and pasta; bring to a boil over high heat. Reduce heat to low; cook 5 minutes.

2. Stir in zucchini; cook 5 to 7 minutes or until pasta and vegetables are tender.

3. Stir in tomatoes; cook until heated through. Top with cheese, basil and pepper.

Vegetable Beef Noodle Soup

1 tablespoon olive oil

8 ounces beef for stew, cut into ½-inch pieces

¾ cup unpeeled cubed potato (1 medium)

½ cup sliced carrot

1 tablespoon balsamic vinegar

¾ teaspoon dried thyme

¼ teaspoon black pepper

2½ cups beef broth

1 cup water

¼ cup chili sauce or ketchup

2 ounces uncooked thin egg noodles

¾ cup jarred or canned pearl onions, rinsed and drained

¼ cup frozen peas

1. Heat oil in large saucepan over medium-high heat. Add beef; cook about 3 minutes or until browned on all sides, stirring occasionally. Remove to plate.

2. Add potato, carrot, vinegar, thyme and pepper to saucepan; cook and stir over medium heat 3 minutes. Add broth, water and chili sauce; bring to a boil over medium-high heat. Stir in beef. Reduce heat to medium-low; cover and simmer 30 minutes or until meat is almost fork-tender.

3. Return soup to a boil over medium-high heat. Add noodles; cover and cook 7 to 10 minutes or until noodles are tender, stirring occasionally. Add onions and peas; cook 1 minute or until heated through. Serve immediately.

Minestrone Soup

1 tablespoon olive oil

½ cup chopped onion

1 stalk celery, diced

1 carrot, diced

2 cloves garlic, minced

2 cups vegetable broth

1½ cups water

1 bay leaf

¾ teaspoon salt

½ teaspoon dried basil

½ teaspoon dried oregano

¼ teaspoon dried thyme

¼ teaspoon sugar

Ground black pepper

1 can (about 15 ounces) dark red kidney beans, rinsed and drained

1 can (about 15 ounces) navy beans or cannellini beans, rinsed and drained

1 can (about 14 ounces) diced tomatoes

1 cup diced zucchini (about 1 small)

½ cup uncooked small shell pasta

½ cup frozen cut green beans

¼ cup dry red wine

1 cup packed chopped stemmed fresh spinach

Grated Parmesan cheese (optional)

1. Heat oil in large saucepan or Dutch oven over medium-high heat. Add onion, celery, carrot and garlic; cook and stir 5 to 7 minutes or until vegetables are tender. Add broth, water, bay leaf, salt, basil, oregano, thyme, sugar and pepper; bring to a boil.

2. Stir in kidney beans, navy beans, tomatoes, zucchini, pasta, green beans and wine; cook 10 minutes, stirring occasionally.

3. Add spinach; cook 2 minutes or until pasta and zucchini are tender. Remove and discard bay leaf. Serve with cheese, if desired.

Spinach Noodle Bowl with Ginger

1 container (48 ounces) chicken broth

4 ounces uncooked vermicelli noodles, broken into thirds

1½ cups matchstick carrots

3 ounces snow peas, stemmed and cut into halves

4 cups packed fresh spinach (4 ounces)

1½ cups cooked shrimp or chicken

½ cup finely chopped green onions

1 tablespoon grated fresh ginger

1 teaspoon soy sauce

⅛ to ¼ teaspoon red pepper flakes

1. Bring broth to a boil in large saucepan or Dutch oven over high heat. Add noodles; return to a boil. Cook until al dente (about 2 minutes less than package directions). Add carrots and snow peas; cook 2 minutes or until noodles are tender.

2. Remove from heat; stir in spinach, shrimp, green onions, ginger, soy sauce and red pepper flakes. Let stand 2 minutes before serving.

Onion Soup with Pasta

1 tablespoon olive oil

3 cups sliced onions

3 cloves garlic, minced

½ teaspoon sugar

2 cans (about 14 ounces each) beef broth

1 cup uncooked bowtie pasta

2 tablespoons dry sherry

¼ teaspoon salt

⅛ teaspoon black pepper

Grated Parmesan cheese (optional)

1. Heat oil in large saucepan over medium heat. Add onions and garlic; cover and cook 6 to 8 minutes or until onions are softened, stirring occasionally. Stir in sugar; cook about 15 minutes or until onion mixture is very soft and browned.

2. Add broth to saucepan; bring to a boil. Stir in pasta; cook 9 to 11 minutes or until tender.

3. Stir in sherry, salt and pepper. Serve with cheese, if desired.

Quick Szechuan Vegetable Noodle Soup

2 cans (about 14 ounces each) vegetable broth

2 teaspoons minced garlic

1 teaspoon minced fresh ginger

¼ teaspoon red pepper flakes

1 package (16 ounces) frozen vegetable medley, such as broccoli, carrots, water chestnuts and red bell peppers

2 packages (3 ounces each) ramen noodles, any flavor,* *or* 5 ounces uncooked angel hair pasta, broken in half

3 tablespoons soy sauce

1 tablespoon dark sesame oil

¼ cup thinly sliced green onions

Discard seasoning packets.

1. Combine broth, garlic, ginger and red pepper flakes in large saucepan; bring to a boil over high heat. Add vegetables and noodles; return to a boil. Reduce heat to medium-low; cook 5 to 6 minutes or until vegetables and noodles are tender, stirring occasionally.

2. Stir in soy sauce and sesame oil; cook 3 minutes. Stir in green onions just before serving.

Tip

For a heartier, protein-packed main dish, add 1 package (14 ounces) extra firm tofu, drained and cut into ¾-inch cubes, to the broth mixture with the soy sauce and sesame oil.

Hearty Vegetable Pasta Soup

1 tablespoon vegetable oil

1 onion, chopped

3 cups vegetable broth

1 can (about 14 ounces)
   diced tomatoes

1 medium potato, cubed

2 carrots, sliced

1 stalk celery, sliced

1 teaspoon dried basil

½ teaspoon salt

⅛ teaspoon black pepper

⅓ cup uncooked mini
   bowtie pasta

2 ounces fresh spinach,
   stemmed and chopped

1. Heat oil in large saucepan or Dutch oven over medium-high heat. Add onion; cook and stir until translucent. Add broth, tomatoes, potato, carrots, celery, basil, salt and pepper; bring to a boil over high heat. Reduce heat to medium-low; simmer, uncovered, 20 minutes or until potato and carrots are very tender, stirring occasionally.

2. Stir in pasta; cook 8 minutes or until pasta is tender.

3. Stir in spinach; cook 2 minutes or until spinach is wilted. Serve immediately.

Quick and Easy Ravioli Soup

8 ounces mild Italian sausage, casings removed

½ cup chopped onion

1 clove garlic, crushed

2 cans (about 14 ounces each) chicken broth

2 cups water

1 package (9 ounces) frozen mini cheese-filled ravioli

1 can (about 15 ounces) chickpeas, rinsed and drained

1 can (about 14 ounces) diced tomatoes with mild green chiles

¾ teaspoon dried oregano

½ teaspoon black pepper

1 cup baby spinach

Grated Parmesan cheese

1. Cook sausage, onion and garlic in large saucepan or Dutch oven over medium heat 5 minutes, stirring to break up meat. Remove sausage mixture to plate. Drain fat.

2. Add broth and water to saucepan; bring to a boil over medium-high heat. Add ravioli; cook 4 to 5 minutes or until tender.

3. Stir in sausage mixture, chickpeas, tomatoes, oregano and pepper; cook until heated through. Stir in spinach; cook 1 minute or until wilted. Sprinkle with cheese.

BEANS & GRAINS

Sausage Rice Soup

2 teaspoons olive oil

8 ounces Italian sausage, casings removed

1 small onion, chopped

½ teaspoon fennel seeds

1 tablespoon tomato paste

4 cups chicken broth

1 can (about 14 ounces) whole tomatoes, undrained, crushed with hands or chopped

1½ cups water

½ cup uncooked rice

¼ teaspoon salt

⅛ teaspoon black pepper

2 to 3 ounces baby spinach

⅓ cup shredded mozzarella cheese (optional)

1. Heat oil in large saucepan or Dutch oven over medium-high heat. Add sausage; cook about 8 minutes or until browned, stirring to break up meat into bite-size pieces. Add onion; cook and stir 5 minutes or until softened. Add fennel seeds; cook and stir 30 seconds. Add tomato paste; cook and stir 1 minute.

2. Stir in broth, tomatoes with juice, water, rice, ¼ teaspoon salt and ⅛ teaspoon pepper; bring to a boil. Reduce heat to medium-low; simmer about 18 minutes or until rice is tender. Stir in spinach; cook about 3 minutes or until wilted. Season with additional salt and pepper.

3. Sprinkle with cheese, if desired, just before serving.

Hearty White Bean Soup

2⅔ cups water, divided

1 can (about 15 ounces) Great Northern beans or navy beans, rinsed and drained

1 cup chicken broth

1 cup chopped carrots

1 cup chopped green or red bell pepper

½ cup chopped celery

2 tablespoons chopped fresh thyme *or* 2 teaspoons dried thyme

2 tablespoons chopped fresh marjoram *or* 2 teaspoons dried marjoram

½ teaspoon ground cumin

¼ teaspoon black pepper

3 tablespoons all-purpose flour

1. Combine 2⅓ cups water, beans, broth, carrots, bell pepper, celery, thyme, marjoram, cumin and black pepper in large saucepan; bring to a boil over high heat. Reduce heat to medium-low; cover and simmer 20 to 25 minutes or until vegetables are tender, stirring occasionally.

2. Stir remaining ⅓ cup water into flour in small bowl until smooth. Add to mixture in saucepan; cook and stir over medium heat until soup boils and thickens. Cook and stir 1 minute.

Chicken, Barley and Vegetable Soup

MAKES 6 SERVINGS

8 ounces boneless skinless chicken breasts, cut into ½-inch pieces

8 ounces boneless skinless chicken thighs, cut into ½-inch pieces

¾ teaspoon salt

¼ teaspoon black pepper

1 tablespoon olive oil

½ cup uncooked pearl barley

4 cans (about 14 ounces each) chicken broth

2 cups water

1 bay leaf

2 cups whole baby carrots

2 cups diced peeled potatoes

2 cups sliced mushrooms

2 cups frozen peas

3 tablespoons sour cream

1 tablespoon chopped fresh dill
  or 1 teaspoon dried dill weed

1. Sprinkle chicken with salt and pepper. Heat oil in large saucepan over medium-high heat. Add chicken; cook without stirring 2 minutes or until golden brown. Turn chicken; cook 2 minutes. Remove to plate.

2. Add barley to saucepan; cook and stir 1 to 2 minutes or until barley begins to brown, adding 1 tablespoon broth, if necessary, to prevent burning. Add remaining broth, water and bay leaf; bring to a boil. Reduce heat to low; cover and simmer 30 minutes.

3. Add chicken, carrots, potatoes and mushrooms; cook 10 minutes or until vegetables are tender. Add peas; cook 2 minutes. Remove and discard bay leaf.

4. Top with sour cream and dill; serve immediately.

Smoky Navy Bean Soup

3 tablespoons olive oil, divided

4 ounces Canadian bacon or ham, diced

1 cup diced onion

1 carrot, thinly sliced

1 stalk celery, thinly sliced

3 cups water

6 ounces red potatoes, diced

2 bay leaves

¼ teaspoon dried tarragon

1 can (about 15 ounces) navy beans, rinsed and drained

1½ teaspoons liquid smoke

½ teaspoon salt

½ teaspoon black pepper

1. Heat 1 tablespoon oil in large saucepan over medium-high heat. Add Canadian bacon; cook and stir 2 minutes or until browned. Remove to plate.

2. Add 1 tablespoon oil, onion, carrot and celery to saucepan; cook and stir 4 minutes or until onion is translucent. Add water; bring to a boil. Stir in potatoes, bay leaves and tarragon. Reduce heat to medium-low; cover and simmer 20 minutes or until potatoes are tender.

3. Stir in beans, Canadian bacon, remaining 1 tablespoon oil, liquid smoke, salt and pepper; cook until heated through. Remove and discard bay leaves.

Middle Eastern Lentil Soup

2 tablespoons olive oil

1 small onion, chopped

1 medium red bell pepper, chopped

1 teaspoon whole fennel seeds

½ teaspoon ground cumin

¼ teaspoon ground red pepper

4 cups water

1 cup dried lentils, rinsed and sorted

½ teaspoon salt

1 tablespoon lemon juice

½ cup plain yogurt

2 tablespoons chopped fresh parsley

1. Heat oil in large saucepan over medium-high heat. Add onion and bell pepper; cook and stir 5 minutes or until vegetables are tender. Add fennel seeds, cumin and ground red pepper; cook and stir 1 minute.

2. Stir in water, lentils and salt; bring to a boil. Reduce heat to low; cover and simmer 25 to 30 minutes or until lentils are tender. Stir in lemon juice.

3. Top each serving with yogurt; sprinkle with parsley.

Tip

Serve with homemade pita chips. Cut 4 pita bread rounds into 6 wedges each. Toss wedges with 1 tablespoon olive oil and 1 teaspoon coarse salt; spread on large baking sheet. Bake at 350°F 15 minutes or until lightly browned and crisp.

Hot Gazpacho Bean Soup

1 tablespoon olive oil

1 cup chopped onion

1 cup chopped green
   bell pepper

1 clove garlic, minced

2 cans (11½ ounces each)
   vegetable juice

1 can (about 15 ounces) red
   kidney beans, rinsed
   and drained

1 can (about 15 ounces)
   chickpeas, rinsed
   and drained

2 cubes beef bouillon

2 tablespoons lemon juice

¼ teaspoon red pepper flakes

3 cups chopped tomatoes,
   divided

1 cup chopped cucumber

½ cup sliced green onions

½ cup plain salad croutons

1. Heat oil in medium saucepan over medium-high heat. Add onion, bell pepper and garlic; cook and stir 4 minutes or until vegetables are crisp-tender.

2. Add vegetable juice, beans, chickpeas, bouillon, lemon juice, red pepper flakes and 1½ cups tomatoes; bring to a boil. Reduce heat to low; cover and simmer 5 minutes.

3. Divide bean mixture among serving bowls. Top with remaining tomatoes, cucumber, green onions and croutons.

Split Pea Soup with Ham and Ale

1 tablespoon olive oil

1 cup chopped onion

½ cup chopped carrot

½ cup chopped celery

3 cloves garlic, minced

1 bay leaf

¼ teaspoon dried thyme

1 bottle (12 ounces) Belgian white ale

4 cups chicken broth

1 package (16 ounces) dried split peas, rinsed and sorted

1 pound smoked ham hocks

2 cups water

1. Heat oil in large saucepan or Dutch oven over medium heat. Add onion, carrot, celery, garlic, bay leaf and thyme; cook 4 to 5 minutes or until vegetables begin to soften, stirring occasionally. Add ale; bring to boil over medium-high heat. Cook 6 to 7 minutes or until beer is reduced by half.

2. Stir in broth, split peas, ham hocks and water; bring to a boil. Reduce heat to medium-low; cover and simmer about 1 hour or until split peas are tender, stirring occasionally.

3. Remove ham hocks to cutting board; let stand until cool enough to handle. Remove ham from hocks. Chop ham and stir into saucepan. Remove and discard bay leaf.

Black Bean Soup

2 tablespoons vegetable oil

1 cup diced onion

1 stalk celery, diced

2 carrots, diced

½ small green bell pepper, diced

4 cloves garlic, minced

4 cans (about 15 ounces each) black beans, rinsed and drained, divided

1 container (32 ounces) vegetable broth, divided

2 tablespoons cider vinegar

2 teaspoons chili powder

½ teaspoon salt

½ teaspoon ground red pepper

½ teaspoon ground cumin

¼ teaspoon liquid smoke

Optional toppings: sour cream, chopped green onions and shredded Cheddar cheese

1. Heat oil in large saucepan or Dutch oven over medium-low heat. Add onion, celery, carrots, bell pepper and garlic; cook 10 minutes, stirring occasionally.

2. Combine half of beans and 1 cup broth in food processor or blender; process until smooth. Add to vegetables in saucepan.

3. Stir in remaining beans, remaining broth, vinegar, chili powder, salt, red pepper, cumin and liquid smoke; bring to a boil over high heat. Reduce heat to medium-low; simmer 1 hour or until vegetables are tender and soup is thickened. Serve with desired toppings.

Mushroom Barley Soup

2 tablespoons butter

8 ounces sliced mushrooms

½ cup chopped onion

½ cup chopped carrots

1 clove garlic, minced

1 teaspoon dried thyme

¼ teaspoon black pepper

¼ cup dry white wine

4 cups chicken broth

¾ cup quick-cooking barley

1. Melt butter in large saucepan over medium-high heat. Add mushrooms, onion, carrots, garlic, thyme and pepper; cook and stir 6 to 8 minutes or until mushrooms begin to brown. Add wine, scraping up browned bits from botom of saucepan.

2. Stir in broth; bring to a boil over high heat. Stir in barley. Reduce heat to low; simmer, partially covered, 15 minutes or until barley is tender.

Tips

For extra flavor, use a mix of button and baby bella mushrooms. For a vegetarian soup, substitute vegetable broth for the chicken broth.

Black-Eyed Pea Soup

2 large potatoes

4 medium onions, thinly sliced

4 carrots, thinly sliced

8 ounces bacon, diced

8 quarts (32 cups) water

2 pounds dried black-eyed peas, rinsed and sorted

2 cups thinly sliced celery

1 meaty ham bone

2 jalapeño peppers*

4 bay leaves

½ teaspoon dried thyme

Salt and black pepper

Jalapeño peppers can sting and irritate the skin, so wear rubber gloves when handling peppers and do not touch your eyes.

1. Peel and grate potatoes. Place grated potatoes in large bowl of cold water; set aside.

2. Combine onions, carrots and bacon in large stockpot or Dutch oven; cook over medium-high heat until onions are golden brown, stirring occasionally.

3. Drain potatoes. Add potatoes, water, black-eyed peas, celery, ham bone, jalapeños, bay leaves and thyme to onion mixture; season with salt and black pepper. Reduce heat to low; cover and simmer 3 to 4 hours or until black-eyed peas are tender. Remove and discard jalapeños and bay leaves.

4. Remove ham bone to cutting board; let stand until cool enough to handle. Remove ham from bone. Chop ham and stir into soup.

Greek Lemon and Rice Soup

2 tablespoons butter

⅓ cup minced green onions

6 cups chicken broth

⅔ cup uncooked long grain rice

4 eggs

Juice of 1 fresh lemon

⅛ teaspoon white pepper (optional)

Fresh mint leaves and lemon peel (optional)

1. Melt butter in medium saucepan over medium heat. Add green onions; cook and stir about 3 minutes or until tender.

2. Stir in broth and rice; bring to a boil over medium-high heat. Reduce heat to low; cover and simmer 20 to 25 minutes or until rice is tender.

3. Beat eggs in medium bowl. Stir in lemon juice and ½ cup hot broth mixture until blended. Gradually pour egg mixture into broth mixture in saucepan, stirring constantly. Cook and stir over low heat 2 to 3 minutes or until soup thickens enough to lightly coat spoon. *Do not boil.*

4. Stir in pepper, if desired. Garnish with mint and lemon peel.

Chickpea-Vegetable Soup

1 tablespoon olive oil

1 cup chopped onion

½ cup chopped green
    bell pepper

2 cloves garlic, minced

2 cans (about 14 ounces each)
    diced tomatoes

3 cups water

2 cups broccoli florets

1 can (about 15 ounces)
    chickpeas, rinsed, drained
    and slightly mashed

½ cup (3 ounces) uncooked orzo
    or rosamarina pasta

1 bay leaf

1 tablespoon chopped fresh
    thyme *or* 1 teaspoon
    dried thyme

1 tablespoon chopped fresh
    rosemary leaves *or*
    1 teaspoon dried rosemary

1 tablespoon lime or lemon juice

½ teaspoon salt

½ teaspoon ground turmeric

¼ teaspoon ground red pepper

¼ cup pumpkin seeds or
    sunflower kernels

1. Heat oil in large saucepan over medium heat. Add onion, bell pepper and garlic; cook and stir 5 minutes or until vegetables are tender.

2. Add tomatoes, water, broccoli, chickpeas, orzo, bay leaf, thyme, rosemary, lime juice, salt, turmeric, and red pepper; bring to a boil over high heat. Reduce heat to medium-low; cover and simmer 10 to 12 minutes or until orzo is tender.

3. Remove and discard bay leaf. Top with pumpkin seeds.

VEGETABLES

Curried Ginger Pumpkin Soup

MAKES 8 SERVINGS

1 tablespoon vegetable oil

1 large sweet onion (such as Walla Walla), coarsely chopped

1 large Golden Delicious apple, peeled and coarsely chopped

3 slices (¼-inch) peeled fresh ginger

1½ teaspoons curry powder

2½ to 3 cups chicken broth, divided

2 cans (15 ounces each) pure pumpkin

1 cup half-and-half

1 teaspoon salt

Black pepper

Roasted salted pumpkin seeds (optional)

1. Heat oil in large saucepan over medium heat. Add onion, apple, ginger and curry powder; cook and stir 10 minutes. Add ½ cup broth; cover and simmer 10 minutes or until apple is tender.

2. Pour onion mixture into blender; blend until smooth. Return to saucepan. (Or use hand-held immersion blender.)

3. Add pumpkin, 2 cups broth, half-and-half, salt and pepper; cook until heated through, stirring occasionally. If soup is too thick, add additional broth, a few tablespoons at a time, until soup reaches desired consistency. Sprinkle with pumpkin seeds, if desired.

Creamy Roasted Poblano Soup

6 large poblano peppers

1 tablespoon olive oil

¾ cup chopped onion

½ cup thinly sliced celery

½ cup thinly sliced carrots

1 clove garlic, minced

2 cans (about 14 ounces each) chicken broth

1 package (8 ounces) cream cheese, cubed

Salt and black pepper

1. Preheat broiler. Line baking sheet with foil. Place poblano peppers on baking sheet; broil 5 to 6 inches from heat source 15 minutes or until peppers are blistered and beginning to char, turning occasionally. Place peppers in medium bowl; cover with plastic wrap. Let stand 20 minutes.

2. Meanwhile, heat oil in large saucepan over medium-high heat. Add onion, celery, carrots and garlic; cook and stir 4 minutes or until onion is translucent. Add broth; bring to a boil. Reduce heat to medium-low; cover and simmer 12 minutes or until celery is tender.

3. Remove skins, stems and seeds from peppers. Briefly run peppers under cold running water to help remove skins and seeds, if necessary. (This removes some smoky flavor, so work quickly.) Add peppers to broth mixture.

4. Working in batches, process broth mixture and cream cheese in food processor or blender until smooth; return to saucepan. (Or use hand-held immersion blender.) Cook and stir over medium heat 2 minutes or until heated through. Season with salt and black pepper.

Sweet Potato Bisque

1 pound sweet potatoes, peeled and cut into 2-inch pieces

1 tablespoon butter

½ cup finely chopped onion

1 teaspoon curry powder

½ teaspoon salt

½ teaspoon ground coriander

⅔ cup unsweetened apple juice

1 cup buttermilk

¼ cup water (optional)

Snipped fresh chives (optional)

Plain yogurt (optional)

1. Place sweet potatoes in large saucepan; cover with water. Bring to a boil over high heat. Cook 15 minutes or until fork-tender. Drain sweet potatoes; cool under cold running water.

2. Meanwhile, melt butter in small saucepan over medium heat. Add onion; cook and stir 2 minutes. Add curry powder, salt and coriander; cook and stir 1 minute or until onion is tender. Remove from heat; stir in apple juice.

3. Combine sweet potatoes, buttermilk and onion mixture in food processor or blender; process until smooth. Return to large saucepan; stir in ¼ cup water, if necessary, to thin to desired consistency. Cook and stir over medium heat until heated through. *Do not boil.* Garnish with chives or yogurt.

Cream of Broccoli Soup

1 bunch broccoli (about 1½ pounds), plus additional for garnish

3 cups chicken broth

1 potato, peeled and chopped

1 medium onion, chopped

1 carrot, chopped

1 stalk celery, chopped

1 clove garlic, minced

½ teaspoon dried basil

2 tablespoons butter

2 tablespoons all-purpose flour

1½ cups milk

1 cup half-and-half

½ cup (2 ounces) shredded Cheddar cheese, plus additional for garnish

½ teaspoon salt

¼ teaspoon black pepper

1. Trim leaves and ends of broccoli stalks. Peel stalks; cut broccoli into ½-inch pieces.

2. Combine broth, potato, onion, carrot, celery, garlic and basil in large saucepan; bring to a boil over high heat. Reduce heat to low; simmer 10 minutes. Add prepared broccoli to saucepan; simmer 10 minutes or until vegetables are fork-tender. Let stand at room temperature 20 minutes to cool slightly. *Do not drain.*

3. Process vegetables in batches in food processor or blender until smooth. (Or use hand-held immersion blender.)

4. Melt butter in Dutch oven or large saucepan over medium heat. Add flour; stir until smooth. Cook 1 minute. Gradually whisk in milk and half-and-half until blended. Stir in ½ cup cheese, salt and pepper. Add puréed vegetable mixture; cook 3 to 5 minutes or until soup thickens, stirring occasionally. Garnish with additional broccoli and cheese.

Baked Potato Soup

3 medium russet potatoes
(about 1 pound)

¼ cup (½ stick) butter

1 cup chopped onion

½ cup all-purpose flour

4 cups chicken or vegetable
broth

1½ cups instant mashed
potato flakes

1 cup water

1 cup half-and-half

1 teaspoon salt

½ teaspoon dried basil

½ teaspoon dried thyme

¼ teaspoon black pepper

1 cup (4 ounces) shredded
Cheddar cheese

4 slices bacon, crisp-cooked
and crumbled

1 green onion, chopped

1. Preheat oven to 400°F. Scrub potatoes and prick in several places with fork. Place in baking pan; bake 1 hour. Cool completely; peel and cut into ½-inch cubes. (Potatoes can be prepared several days in advance; refrigerate until ready to use.)

2. Melt butter in large saucepan or Dutch oven over medium heat. Add onion; cook and stir 3 minutes or until softened. Whisk in flour; cook and stir 1 minute. Gradually whisk in broth until well blended. Stir in mashed potato flakes, water, half-and-half, salt, basil, thyme and pepper; bring to a boil over medium-high heat. Reduce heat to medium; cook 5 minutes.

3. Stir in baked potato cubes; cook 10 to 15 minutes or until soup is thickened and heated through. Top with cheese, bacon and green onion.

Garden Vegetable Soup

1 tablespoon olive oil

1 medium onion, chopped

1 carrot, chopped

1 stalk celery, chopped

1 medium zucchini, diced

1 medium yellow squash, diced

1 red bell pepper, diced

2 tablespoons tomato paste

2 cloves garlic, minced

2 teaspoons salt

1 teaspoon Italian seasoning

½ teaspoon black pepper

8 cups vegetable broth

1 can (28 ounces) whole tomatoes, undrained, chopped

½ cup uncooked pearl barley

1 cup cut green beans (1-inch pieces)

½ cup corn

¼ cup slivered fresh basil

1 tablespoon lemon juice

1. Heat oil in large saucepan or Dutch oven over medium-high heat. Add onion, carrot and celery; cook and stir 8 minutes or until vegetables are softened.

2. Add zucchini, yellow squash and bell pepper; cook and stir 5 minutes or until softened. Stir in tomato paste, garlic, salt, Italian seasoning and black pepper; cook 1 minute. Stir in broth and tomatoes with juice; bring to a boil. Stir in barley.

3. Reduce heat to low; simmer, uncovered, 30 minutes. Stir in green beans and corn; cook about 15 minutes or until barley is tender and green beans are crisp-tender. Stir in basil and lemon juice.

Creamy Tomato Soup

3 tablespoons olive oil, divided

2 tablespoons butter

1 large onion, finely chopped

2 cloves garlic, minced

2 teaspoons sugar

1 teaspoon salt

½ teaspoon dried oregano

2 cans (28 ounces each) peeled Italian plum tomatoes, undrained

½ cup whipping cream

Optional toppings: diced tomatoes, pumpkin seeds, finely chopped fresh parsley, basil, oregano and/or thyme

1. Heat 2 tablespoons oil and butter in large saucepan or Dutch oven over medium-high heat. Add onion; cook and stir 5 minutes or until softened. Add garlic, sugar, salt and oregano; cook and stir 30 seconds. Stir in tomatoes with juice; bring to a boil. Reduce heat to medium-low; simmer, uncovered, 45 minutes, stirring occasionally.

2. Blend soup with hand-held immersion blender until smooth. (Or process soup in batches in food processor or blender.) Stir in cream; cook until heated through. Garnish with desired toppings.

Coconut Cauliflower Cream Soup

- 1 tablespoon coconut or vegetable oil
- 1 medium onion, chopped
- 1 tablespoon minced garlic
- 1 tablespoon minced fresh ginger
- 1 teaspoon salt
- 1 head cauliflower (1½ pounds), cut into florets
- 2 cans (about 13 ounces each) coconut milk, divided
- 1 cup water
- 1 teaspoon garam masala
- ½ teaspoon ground turmeric

  Optional toppings: hot chili oil, red pepper flakes and chopped fresh cilantro

1. Heat oil in large saucepan over medium-high heat. Add onion; cook and stir 5 minutes or until softened. Add garlic, ginger and salt; cook and stir 30 seconds.

2. Add cauliflower, 1 can coconut milk, water, garam masala and turmeric. Reduce heat to medium; cover and simmer 20 minutes or until cauliflower is very tender.

3. Remove from heat. Blend soup with immersion blender until smooth.* Return saucepan to medium heat; add 1 cup coconut milk. Cook and stir until heated through. Add additional coconut milk, if desired, to reach desired consistency. Garnish with chili oil, red pepper flakes and cilantro.

*Or blend soup in batches in blender or food processor. Cool to room temperature first if your appliance should not be used to blend hot liquids.

Harvest Squash Soup

1 acorn squash or sugar pumpkin (about 2 pounds)

1 butternut or kabocha squash (about 2 pounds)

Salt and black pepper

2 tablespoons olive oil

2 tablespoons butter

1 large onion, finely chopped

2 stalks celery, chopped

1 medium carrot, chopped

¼ cup packed brown sugar

2 tablespoons tomato paste

1 tablespoon minced fresh ginger

1 clove garlic, minced

1 teaspoon salt

1 teaspoon ground cinnamon

¼ teaspoon ground cumin

¼ teaspoon black pepper

4 cups vegetable broth

1 cup milk

2 teaspoons lemon juice

Roasted pumpkin seeds (optional)

1. Preheat oven to 400°F. Line large baking sheet with foil; spray with nonstick cooking spray.

2. Cut squash in half; remove and discard seeds and strings. Season cut sides with salt and pepper. Place cut sides down on prepared baking sheet; bake 30 to 45 minutes or until fork-tender. When squash is cool enough to handle, remove skin; chop flesh into 1-inch pieces.

3. Heat oil and butter in large saucepan or Dutch oven over medium-high heat. Add onion, celery and carrot; cook and stir 5 minutes or until vegetables are tender. Add brown sugar, tomato paste, ginger, garlic, 1 teaspoon salt, cinnamon, cumin and ¼ teaspoon pepper; cook and stir 1 minute. Stir in broth and squash; bring to a boil. Reduce heat to medium; cook 20 minutes or until squash is very soft.

4. Blend soup with immersion blender until desired consistency. (Or process in batches in food processor or blender.) Stir in milk and lemon juice; cook until heated through. Garnish with pumpkin seeds.

Broccoli Cheese Soup

6 tablespoons (¾ stick) butter

1 cup chopped onion

1 clove garlic, minced

¼ cup all-purpose flour

2 cups vegetable broth

2 cups milk

1½ teaspoons Dijon mustard

½ teaspoon salt

¼ teaspoon ground nutmeg

¼ teaspoon black pepper

⅛ teaspoon hot pepper sauce

1 package (16 ounces) frozen broccoli (5 cups)

2 carrots, shredded (1 cup)

6 ounces pasteurized process cheese product, cubed

1 cup (4 ounces) shredded sharp Cheddar cheese, plus additional for garnish

1. Melt butter in large saucepan or Dutch oven over medium-low heat. Add onion; cook and stir 8 minutes or until softened. Add garlic; cook and stir 1 minute. Increase heat to medium. Whisk in flour until smooth; cook and stir 3 minutes without browning.

2. Gradually whisk in broth and milk. Add mustard, salt, nutmeg, black pepper and hot pepper sauce; cook 15 minutes or until thickened, stirring occasionally.

3. Add broccoli; cook 15 minutes. Add carrots; cook 10 minutes or until vegetables are tender.

4. Transfer half of soup to food processor or blender; process until smooth. Return to saucepan. Add cheese product and 1 cup Cheddar; cook and stir over low heat until cheese is melted. Ladle into bowls; garnish with additional Cheddar.

Cream of Asparagus Soup

1 pound asparagus

3½ cups vegetable or chicken broth, divided

¼ cup (½ stick) butter

¼ cup all-purpose flour

½ cup whipping cream

½ teaspoon salt

⅛ teaspoon black pepper

1. Trim off and discard tough ends of asparagus. Cut asparagus into 1-inch pieces. Combine asparagus and 1 cup broth in medium saucepan; cook over medium heat 12 to 15 minutes or until tender.

2. Remove 1 cup asparagus pieces to small bowl. Process remaining asparagus with broth in food processor or blender until smooth.

3. Melt butter in large saucepan over medium heat. Whisk in flour until smooth. Gradually add remaining 1½ cups broth; cook until slightly thickened, stirring occasionally.

4. Stir in cream, salt, pepper, puréed asparagus mixture and reserved asparagus pieces; cook until heated through.

Roasted Butternut Squash Soup

1 butternut squash (about 1½ pounds)

2 tablespoons olive oil, divided

⅔ cup chopped onion

2½ cups vegetable broth

1 Granny Smith apple, peeled and cubed

½ teaspoon salt

¼ teaspoon ground cinnamon

⅛ teaspoon ground nutmeg

⅛ teaspoon black pepper

¼ cup half-and-half

Pumpkin seeds (optional)

1. Preheat oven to 400°F. Line baking sheet with foil. Peel squash; remove and discard seeds and strings. Cut squash into 2-inch cubes. Combine squash and 1 tablespoon oil on prepared baking sheet; toss to coat. Spread in single layer. Roast 14 minutes or until almost tender.

2. Meanwhile, heat remaining 1 tablespoon oil in large saucepan over medium heat. Add onion; cook and stir 5 minutes until soft and lightly browned. Add broth, apple and salt; bring to a boil over high heat. Reduce heat to low; cover and simmer 10 minutes.

3. Add squash; cover and simmer 5 minutes or until tender. Remove from heat; process in batches in food processor or blender until smooth. (Or use hand-held immersion blender.) Return to saucepan; stir in cinnamon, nutmeg and pepper. Simmer, uncovered, 3 minutes. Stir in half-and-half. Sprinkle with pumpkin seeds, if desired. Serve immediately.

WEEKNIGHT WONDERS

Salsa Verde Chicken Soup

MAKES 4 TO 6 SERVINGS

1 tablespoon vegetable oil

1½ pounds boneless skinless chicken breasts, cut into ¾-inch pieces

2 cans (about 15 ounces each) black beans, rinsed and drained

1 jar (24 ounces) salsa verde

1½ cups frozen corn

¾ cup chopped fresh cilantro

Diced avocado (optional)

1. Heat oil in large saucepan over medium-high heat. Add chicken; cook and stir about 5 minutes or until chicken begins to brown.

2. Stir in beans and salsa; bring to a simmer. Reduce heat to low; cover and cook 8 minutes.

3. Stir in corn; cook, uncovered, about 3 minutes or until heated through. Remove from heat; stir in cilantro. Garnish with avocado.

One-Pot Chinese Chicken Soup

6 cups chicken broth

2 cups water

1 pound boneless skinless chicken thighs

⅓ cup reduced-sodium soy sauce

1 package (16 ounces) frozen stir-fry vegetables

6 ounces uncooked dried thin Chinese egg noodles

1 to 3 tablespoons sriracha sauce

1. Combine broth, water, chicken and soy sauce in medium saucepan; bring to a boil over high heat. Reduce heat to low; cover and simmer about 20 minutes or until chicken is cooked through and very tender. Remove to bowl; let stand until cool enough to handle.

2. Meanwhile, add vegetables and noodles to broth in saucepan; bring to a boil over high heat. Reduce heat to medium-high; cook about 5 minutes or until noodles are tender and vegetables are heated through, stirring frequently.

3. Shred chicken into bite-size pieces. Stir chicken and 1 tablespoon sriracha into soup; taste and add additional sriracha for spicier flavor.

Roman Spinach Soup

6 cups chicken broth

4 eggs

¼ cup minced fresh basil

3 tablespoons grated Parmesan cheese

2 tablespoons fresh lemon juice

1 tablespoon minced fresh parsley

¼ teaspoon white pepper

⅛ teaspoon ground nutmeg

8 cups packed stemmed fresh spinach, chopped

1. Bring broth to a boil in large saucepan over medium heat.

2. Beat eggs, basil, cheese, lemon juice, parsley, pepper and nutmeg in small bowl until well blended.

3. Stir spinach into broth; cook 1 minute. Slowly pour egg mixture into broth, whisking constantly to form egg threads. Cook 2 to 3 minutes or until egg is cooked. Serve immediately.

Note

Soup may look curdled.

Picante Black Bean Soup

4 slices bacon, cut into ½-inch pieces

1 large onion, chopped

1 clove garlic, minced

2 cans (about 15 ounces each) black beans, undrained

1 can (about 14 ounces) beef broth

1¼ cups water

¾ cup picante sauce, plus additional for serving

½ to 1 teaspoon salt

½ teaspoon dried oregano

Sour cream

1. Cook bacon in large saucepan over medium-high heat until crisp, stirring frequently. Drain on paper towel-lined plate.

2. Add onion and garlic to drippings in saucepan; cook and stir 3 minutes. Stir in beans with liquid, broth, water, ¾ cup picante sauce, ½ teaspoon salt and oregano; bring to a boil. Reduce heat to low; cover and simmer 20 minutes. Taste and adjust seasoning, if desired.

3. Top each serving with sour cream; sprinkle with bacon. Serve with additional picante sauce.

Spicy Thai Coconut Soup

2   cups chicken broth

1   can (about 13 ounces)
    light coconut milk

1   tablespoon minced
    fresh ginger

½   to 1 teaspoon red curry paste

3   cups coarsely shredded
    cooked chicken
    (about 12 ounces)

1   can (15 ounces) straw
    mushrooms, drained

1   can (about 8 ounces)
    baby corn, drained

2   tablespoons lime juice

¼   cup chopped fresh cilantro

1. Combine broth, coconut milk, ginger and curry paste in large saucepan. Add chicken, mushrooms and corn. Bring to a simmer over medium heat; cook until heated through.

2. Stir in lime juice. Sprinkle with cilantro before serving.

Note

Red curry paste can be found in jars in the Asian food section of large grocery stores. Spice levels can vary between brands, so start with ½ teaspoon, then add more as desired.

Quick Tuscan Bean, Tomato and Spinach Soup

2 cans (about 14 ounces each) diced tomatoes with onions

1 can (about 14 ounces) chicken broth

2 teaspoons sugar

2 teaspoons dried basil

¾ teaspoon Worcestershire sauce

1 can (about 15 ounces) small white beans, rinsed and drained

3 ounces baby spinach or chopped stemmed fresh spinach

1 tablespoon extra virgin olive oil

1. Combine tomatoes, broth, sugar, basil and Worcestershire sauce in large saucepan or Dutch oven; bring to a boil over high heat. Reduce heat to low; simmer, uncovered, 10 minutes.

2. Stir in beans and spinach; cook 5 minutes or until spinach is tender.

3. Remove from heat; stir in oil just before serving.

Miso Soup with Tofu

½ cup dried bonito flakes*

4 cups chicken broth

2 teaspoons vegetable oil

1 leek, white part only, finely chopped

1 tablespoon white miso**

8 ounces firm tofu, cut into ½-inch cubes (about 1½ cups)

Dried bonito flakes (katsuobushi) are available in the Asian section of large supermarkets or in Asian stores. If unavailable, use all chicken broth and add an additional 1 tablespoon miso.

**Miso is fermented soybean paste used frequently in Japanese cooking. Miso comes in many varieties; the light yellow miso, usually labeled "white", is the mildest. Look for it in tubs or plastic pouches in the produce section or Asian aisle of the supermarket.*

1. Combine bonito flakes and broth in medium saucepan; bring to a boil over medium heat. Strain out bonito, reserving broth.

2. Heat oil in medium saucepan over medium heat. Add leek; cook 2 to 3 minutes or until tender, stirring frequently.

3. Return broth to saucepan. Add miso; stir until well blended. Add tofu; cook over low heat just until heated through.

Cream-Cheesy Garden Chowder

1 can (about 14 ounces) chicken broth

2 cups frozen corn

2 cups frozen diced hash brown potatoes

8 ounces frozen chopped green bell peppers

½ teaspoon dried thyme

1 teaspoon seafood seasoning

⅛ teaspoon red pepper flakes (optional)

½ cup milk

2 ounces cream cheese, cut into small pieces

½ teaspoon salt

Black pepper

1. Bring broth to a boil in large saucepan over high heat. Add corn, potatoes, bell peppers, thyme, seafood seasoning and red pepper flakes, if desired; return to a boil. Reduce heat to low; cover and simmer 15 minutes or until bell peppers are tender.

2. Remove from heat; whisk in milk, cream cheese, salt and black pepper until cream cheese is melted. Let stand 5 minutes before serving.

French Lentil Soup

3 tablespoons olive oil

1 medium onion, chopped

1 carrot, chopped

1 stalk celery, chopped

1 clove garlic, minced

8 ounces dried lentils, rinsed and sorted

3 cups chicken broth

1 can (about 14 ounces) stewed tomatoes

2 tablespoons balsamic vinegar

1 teaspoon salt

Black pepper

½ cup grated Parmesan cheese (optional)

1. Heat oil in large skillet over medium heat. Add onion, carrot, celery and garlic; cook 8 minutes or until vegetables are tender but not browned, stirring occasionally.

2. Stir in lentils, broth, tomatoes, vinegar and salt; bring to a boil over high heat. Reduce heat to low; cover and simmer 30 minutes or lentils are until tender.

3. Season with pepper; serve with cheese, if desired.

Hot and Sour Soup

2 cans (about 14 ounces each) chicken broth

1 can (4 ounces) sliced mushrooms

2 tablespoons rice vinegar or white wine vinegar

¼ to ½ teaspoon hot pepper sauce

2 tablespoons soy sauce

2 tablespoons cornstarch

1 egg, lightly beaten

2 green onions, thinly sliced, plus additional for garnish

Thinly sliced red chile pepper (optional)

1. Combine broth, mushrooms, vinegar and hot pepper sauce in medium saucepan; bring to a boil over high heat.

2. Stir soy sauce into cornstarch in small bowl until smooth. Add to saucepan; stir over medium-high heat until soup is slightly thickened.

3. Slowly pour in egg, whisking constantly in one direction 1 minute or until egg is cooked. Remove from heat; stir in 2 green onions. Garnish with additional green onion and chile pepper.

Tip

For a heartier soup, add shredded cooked chicken to the broth before thickening it.

Chicken Tortellini Soup

6 cups chicken broth

1 package (9 ounces) refrigerated cheese and spinach tortellini

1 package (about 6 ounces) refrigerated fully cooked chicken breast strips, cut into bite-size pieces

2 cups baby spinach

4 to 6 tablespoons grated Parmesan cheese

1 tablespoon chopped fresh chives *or* 2 tablespoons sliced green onion

1. Bring broth to a boil in large saucepan over high heat; add tortellini. Reduce heat to medium; cook 5 minutes. Stir in chicken and spinach.

2. Reduce heat to low; cook 3 minutes or until chicken is heated through. Sprinkle with cheese and chives.

SLOW COOKER SOUPS

Vegetable and Red Lentil Soup

1 can (about 14 ounces) vegetable broth

1 can (about 14 ounces) diced tomatoes

2 medium zucchini or yellow squash (or 1 of each), chopped

1 red or yellow bell pepper, chopped

½ cup thinly sliced carrots

½ cup dried red lentils, rinsed and sorted*

½ teaspoon salt

½ teaspoon sugar

¼ teaspoon black pepper

2 tablespoons chopped fresh basil or thyme

½ cup croutons (optional)

If you have difficulty finding red lentils, substitute dried brown lentils.

1. Combine broth, tomatoes, zucchini, bell pepper, carrots, lentils, salt, sugar and black pepper in slow cooker; mix well.

2. Cover; cook on LOW 8 hours or on HIGH 4 hours. Top with basil and croutons, if desired.

Chicken and Barley Soup

1 cup thinly sliced celery

1 medium onion, coarsely chopped

1 carrot, thinly sliced

½ cup uncooked medium pearl barley

1 clove garlic, minced

1 cut-up whole chicken (about 3 pounds)

1 tablespoon olive oil

2½ cups chicken broth

1 can (about 14 ounces) diced tomatoes

¾ teaspoon salt

½ teaspoon dried basil

¼ teaspoon black pepper

1. Combine celery, onion, carrot, barley and garlic in slow cooker; mix well.

2. Remove and discard skin from chicken. Separate drumsticks from thighs. Trim backbone from breasts. Save wings for another use. Heat oil in large skillet over medium-high heat; brown chicken on all sides. Place in slow cooker; add broth, tomatoes, salt, basil and pepper.

3. Cover; cook on LOW 7 to 8 hours or HIGH 4 hours or until chicken and barley are tender. Remove chicken to large plate; let stand until cool enough to handle.

4. Remove chicken meat from bones; discard bones. Cut chicken into bite-size pieces; stir into soup.

Easy Corn Chowder

2 cans (about 14 ounces each) chicken broth

1 bag (16 ounces) frozen corn, thawed

3 small potatoes, peeled and cut into ½-inch pieces

1 red bell pepper, diced

1 medium onion, diced

1 stalk celery, sliced

½ teaspoon salt

½ teaspoon black pepper

¼ teaspoon ground coriander

½ cup whipping cream

4 slices bacon, crisp-cooked and crumbled (optional)

1. Combine broth, corn, potatoes, bell pepper, onion, celery, salt, black pepper and coriander in slow cooker; mix well.

2. Cover; cook on LOW 7 to 8 hours. Partially mash soup mixture with potato masher to thicken. Stir in cream; cook on HIGH, uncovered, until hot. Adjust seasonings. Top with bacon, if desired.

Beef Fajita Soup

1 pound cubed beef stew meat

1 can (about 15 ounces) pinto beans, rinsed and drained

1 can (about 15 ounces) black beans, rinsed and drained

1 can (about 14 ounces) diced tomatoes with roasted garlic

1 can (about 14 ounces) beef broth

1½ cups water

1 green bell pepper, thinly sliced

1 red bell pepper, thinly sliced

1 onion, thinly sliced

2 teaspoons ground cumin

1 teaspoon seasoned salt

1 teaspoon black pepper

Optional toppings: sour cream, shredded Monterey Jack or Cheddar cheese, chopped olives

1. Combine beef, beans, tomatoes, broth, water, bell peppers, onion, cumin, seasoned salt and black pepper in slow cooker; mix well.

2. Cover; cook on LOW 8 hours. Serve with desired toppings.

Potato Cheddar Soup

2 pounds new red potatoes, unpeeled and cut into ½-inch pieces

3 cups chicken or vegetable broth

1 medium onion, coarsely chopped

¾ cup coarsely chopped carrots

½ teaspoon salt

1 cup half-and-half

¼ teaspoon black pepper

2 cups (8 ounces) shredded Cheddar cheese

Seasoned croutons (optional)

1. Combine potatoes, broth, onion, carrots and salt in slow cooker; mix well.

2. Cover; cook on LOW 6 to 7 hours or on HIGH 3 to 3½ hours or until vegetables are tender.

3. Stir in half-and-half and pepper. Cover; cook on HIGH 15 minutes. Turn off heat. Let stand, uncovered, 5 minutes. Stir in cheese until melted. Top with croutons, if desired.

Lime
and Black
Bean Soup

2 cans (about 15 ounces each) reduced-sodium black beans, undrained

1 can (about 14 ounces) chicken broth

1½ cups chopped onions

1½ teaspoons chili powder

¾ teaspoon ground cumin

¼ teaspoon garlic powder

⅛ to ¼ teaspoon red pepper flakes

½ cup sour cream

2 tablespoons extra virgin olive oil

2 tablespoons chopped fresh cilantro

1 lime, cut into wedges

1. Combine beans with liquid, broth, onions, chili powder, cumin, garlic powder and red pepper flakes in slow cooker; mix well.

2. Cover; cook on LOW 7 hours or on HIGH 3½ hours or until onions are very soft.

3. Transfer half of soup mixture to food processor or blender; process until smooth. Stir into slow cooker. Turn off heat; let stand 15 to 20 minutes before serving. Top with sour cream, oil and cilantro; serve with lime wedges.

Provençal Lentil Rice Soup

6 cups vegetable broth

1 cup dried lentils, rinsed and sorted

2 carrots, finely diced

1 onion, finely chopped

2 stalks celery, finely diced

3 tablespoons uncooked rice

2 teaspoons minced garlic

1 teaspoon herbes de Provence

½ teaspoon salt

⅛ teaspoon black pepper

4 tablespoons whipping cream or sour cream

¼ cup chopped fresh parsley

1. Combine broth, lentils, carrots, onion, celery, rice, garlic, herbes de Provence, salt and pepper in slow cooker; mix well.

2. Cover; cook on LOW 8 hours or on HIGH 4 hours. Transfer about 1½ cups soup to food processor or blender; process until almost smooth. Stir into slow cooker. Top with cream and parsley.

Mexican Chicken and Black Bean Soup

MAKES 4 SERVINGS

4 bone-in chicken thighs, skin removed

1 can (about 15 ounces) black beans, rinsed and drained

1 can (about 14 ounces) diced tomatoes with Mexican seasoning or diced tomatoes with green chiles

1 can (about 14 ounces) chicken broth

1 cup finely chopped onion

1 cup frozen corn

1 can (4 ounces) chopped mild green chiles

1 tablespoon chili powder

1 teaspoon ground cumin

1 teaspoon salt

Optional toppings: sour cream, sliced avocado, shredded cheese, chopped fresh cilantro, fried tortilla strips

1. Combine chicken, beans, tomatoes, broth, onion, corn, chiles, chili powder, cumin and salt in slow cooker; mix well.

2. Cover; cook on HIGH 3 to 4 hours or until chicken is cooked through. Remove chicken to large plate with slotted spoon. Remove chicken meat from bones; discard bones. Shred chicken into bite-size pieces.

3. Return chicken to slow cooker; mix well. Serve with desired toppings.

Tip

To skin chicken easily, grasp skin with paper towel and pull away. Repeat with fresh paper towel for each piece of chicken.

Simmered Split Pea Soup

3   cans (about 14 ounces each) chicken broth

1   package (16 ounces) dried split peas, rinsed and sorted

1   onion, diced

2   carrots, diced

8   slices bacon, crisp-cooked and crumbled, divided

1   teaspoon black pepper

½   teaspoon dried thyme

1   bay leaf

1. Combine broth, split peas, onion, carrots, half of bacon, pepper, thyme and bay leaf in slow cooker; mix well.

2. Cover; cook on LOW 6 to 8 hours. Remove and discard bay leaf. Adjust seasonings, if desired. Garnish with remaining bacon.

Navy Bean Bacon Chowder

1½ cups dried navy beans, rinsed and drained

2 cups cold water

6 slices thick-cut bacon

1 medium carrot, cut lengthwise into halves, then cut into 1-inch pieces

1 small turnip, cut into 1-inch pieces

1 stalk celery, chopped

1 medium onion, chopped

1 teaspoon Italian seasoning

⅛ teaspoon black pepper

1 container (48 ounces) chicken broth

1 cup milk

1. Soak beans overnight in cold water; drain.

2. Cook bacon in medium skillet over medium heat until crisp. Drain on paper-towel lined plate. Crumble bacon. Combine carrot, turnip, beans, bacon, celery, onion, Italian seasoning and pepper in slow cooker. Stir in broth; mix well.

3. Cover; cook on LOW 8 to 9 hours or until beans are tender. Transfer 2 cups soup mixture to food processor or blender; process until smooth. Stir into slow cooker.

4. Stir in milk. Cover; cook on HIGH 15 minutes or until heated through.

Metric Conversion Chart

VOLUME MEASUREMENTS (dry)

¹/₈ teaspoon = 0.5 mL
¹/₄ teaspoon = 1 mL
¹/₂ teaspoon = 2 mL
³/₄ teaspoon = 4 mL
1 teaspoon = 5 mL
1 tablespoon = 15 mL
2 tablespoons = 30 mL
¹/₄ cup = 60 mL
¹/₃ cup = 75 mL
¹/₂ cup = 125 mL
²/₃ cup = 150 mL
³/₄ cup = 175 mL
1 cup = 250 mL
2 cups = 1 pint = 500 mL
3 cups = 750 mL
4 cups = 1 quart = 1 L

VOLUME MEASUREMENTS (fluid)

1 fluid ounce (2 tablespoons) = 30 mL
4 fluid ounces (¹/₂ cup) = 125 mL
8 fluid ounces (1 cup) = 250 mL
12 fluid ounces (1¹/₂ cups) = 375 mL
16 fluid ounces (2 cups) = 500 mL

WEIGHTS (mass)

¹/₂ ounce = 15 g
1 ounce = 30 g
3 ounces = 90 g
4 ounces = 120 g
8 ounces = 225 g
10 ounces = 285 g
12 ounces = 360 g
16 ounces = 1 pound = 450 g

DIMENSIONS

¹/₁₆ inch = 2 mm
¹/₈ inch = 3 mm
¹/₄ inch = 6 mm
¹/₂ inch = 1.5 cm
³/₄ inch = 2 cm
1 inch = 2.5 cm

OVEN TEMPERATURES

250°F = 120°C
275°F = 140°C
300°F = 150°C
325°F = 160°C
350°F = 180°C
375°F = 190°C
400°F = 200°C
425°F = 220°C
450°F = 230°C

BAKING PAN SIZES

Utensil	Size in Inches/Quarts	Metric Volume	Size in Centimeters
Baking or Cake Pan (square or rectangular)	8×8×2	2 L	20×20×5
	9×9×2	2.5 L	23×23×5
	12×8×2	3 L	30×20×5
	13×9×2	3.5 L	33×23×5
Loaf Pan	8×4×3	1.5 L	20×10×7
	9×5×3	2 L	23×13×7
Round Layer Cake Pan	8×1½	1.2 L	20×4
	9×1½	1.5 L	23×4
Pie Plate	8×1¼	750 mL	20×3
	9×1¼	1 L	23×3
Baking Dish or Casserole	1 quart	1 L	—
	1½ quart	1.5 L	—
	2 quart	2 L	—